The Dream of
Dances With Wolves

The movie *Dances With Wolves* premiered in November 1990 in Washington, D.C., Los Angeles, and South Dakota and, against all odds, became the most highly acclaimed motion picture of the year. It was a dream come true for many of the people who made the film, including Michael Blake, who wrote the screenplay based on his novel.

When Michael Blake accepted the Academy Award for his work on March 25, 1991, he was joined on stage by Doris Leader Charge (see page 130), who was the Lakota language translator and instructor during the movie production. He gave this speech, which she simultaneously translated into Lakota:

"My success began long ago when I began to read books.

"Dreams come out of books and the dream that came to me was...to do something for the benefit of as many people as I could.

"The miracle of *Dances With Wolves*...is that it proves this kind of dream can come true.

"Hold onto fine dreams.
Don't let anyone take them away.
Don't give up."

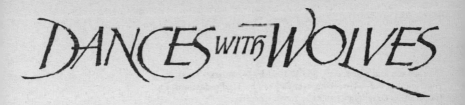

THE ILLUSTRATED SCREENPLAY
AND STORY BEHIND THE FILM
Abridged Edition

KEVIN COSTNER

MICHAEL BLAKE   JIM WILSON

PHOTOGRAPHS BY BEN GLASS

Newmarket Press
New York

This book is an abridged edition of *Dances With Wolves: The Illustrated Story of the Epic Film,*
by Kevin Costner, Michael Blake, and Jim Wilson, published by Newmarket Press, December 1990.

This book published simultaneously in the United States of America and in Canada.

91 92 93 94 10 9 8 7 6 5 4 3 2 1

Newmarket Press gratefully acknowledges permission to reprint material from the following sources:
America's Fascinating Indian Heritage © 1978, The Reader's Digest Association, Inc. Used by
permission. 127.
Kicking Bird, photograph by William S. Soule. Smithsonian Institution, Anthropology Archives. 135.
The Indians by the Editors of Time-Life Books with text by Benjamin Capps. Copyright © 1973 by
Time-Life Books, Inc. Used by permission. 138.

Library of Congress Cataloging-in-Publication Data

Costner, Kevin.
 Dances with wolves : the illustrated screenplay and story behind the film /
Kevin Costner, Michael Blake, Jim Wilson : photographs by Ben Glass.
 — Abridged ed.
  p. cm.
 Summary : Depicts the making of the film "Dances With Wolves."
Includes the screenplay, features about Plains Indians culture, and
information on the historical background.
 ISBN 1-55704-105-9
 ISBN 1-55704-121-0 (special book club paperback)
 1. Dances with wolves (Motion picture)—Juvenile literature.
[1. Dances with wolves (Motion picture). 2. Western films.]
I. Blake, Michael, 1943- . II. Glass, Ben, ill. III. Dances with
wolves (Motion picture) IV. Title.
PN1997.D283C66 1991   91-20284
791.43'72—dc20   CIP
                 AC

Manufactured in the United States of America

Contents

Introduction

So often we think there is a difference between ourselves and the people who are actually in the movies. I would simply say to you that we probably have more in common than you think.

If you have chosen to have this book in your home, it probably means that you are a lover of movies. Knowing that, I feel secure in telling you that this foreword is meant as a personal introduction to both the movie and the thoughts that shaped it.

"Dances With Wolves" is first and foremost a movie, and should be seen as one. The value of this book will never measure up to the first time you experience the movie. Since I know the story, I will forever be jealous of the pureness in which you are able to approach and see it.

With that in mind and off my chest, I can tell you that "Dances With Wolves" was in fact born out of a personal challenge, the seed of which came out of a conflict that could easily have torn the fabric of a long friendship. It will forever be to Michael Blake's credit that "Dances" was conceived and my great luck to be associated with it.

"Dances" as a story began as most stories, with one writer confronting an empty piece of paper. There was no premise. There was no deadline. And out of this freedom came the opportunity to write from the heart.

That Michael would write about the American frontier was in many ways a complete surprise. That I loved it was not. Michael managed to forge all the elements most attractive to me—simplicity, dignity, humor, and poignancy. He created a story that embraced a culture that has traditionally been misrepresented, both historically and cinematically.

That "Dances" was a movie was clear. Whether I should direct this movie was probably the biggest question. It became both a personal and a professional battle. The one thing I knew, however, was that if "Dances" in the smallest way was not as great as the movies that had shaped my love of them, I would always regret my decision.

My only hope is that this movie has an impact on you. It wasn't made to manipulate your feelings, to reinvent the past, or to set the historical record straight. It's a romantic look at a terrible time in our history, when expansion in the name of progress brought us very little and, in fact, cost us deeply.

This book represents the last physical responsibility that I have to the movie, and through it I can reflect on the new friends that were made and the old that stood by me. I think how I have grown up, and now know more than ever the value of my family and the love of my friends.

If I am blessed with good health, there is little doubt that I will make other movies, but if I could not, "Dances With Wolves" would complete the picture I have had of myself since I was a little boy. It will forever be my love letter to the past.

Producer's Notes

I got to know Kevin Costner during the filming in 1981 of "Stacy's Knights," a gambling picture set in Reno that I was directing. I had gone to film school with Michael Blake a few years earlier in Berkeley, and hired him to write the screenplay. It was the first movie I directed and the first he actually got paid to write.

It was also Kevin's first starring role. We'd met a lot of actors for the lead role of Will Bonner, and then Kevin showed up to audition. He'd taken the afternoon off from his job as a stage manager at Raleigh Studios, where our offices are now located. Michael and I and the casting director unanimously agreed that he was the character. That's how we met, but the chance for us all to work together again didn't come for another eight years, until "Dances With Wolves."

I followed the progress of Michael's novel pretty closely. Occasionally he would stay at our house and read chapters to my wife and me. I thought immediately that the character of

Lieutenant Dunbar would be ideal for Kevin, and once he had read the manuscript, he too agreed. There was no one I wanted to produce a film for more than Kevin. I would have done anything to get it done, because I believed in Michael's story and in Kevin's instincts as an actor/director.

Once Kevin made the decision to direct, a critical task was to find the right location for shooting the movie. I needed America in the 1860s, complete with tribes of Native Americans, herds of buffalo and horses, endless prairie vistas with rivers and snow-capped mountains—all within driving distance of a city that could support our crew of 200-plus. Needless to say, we did a lot of flying, scouting locations in eight states as well as Canada and Mexico.

At first I had Oklahoma and Texas in mind, because the Indians in Michael's novel were Comanches and they were indigenous to those areas. That's one item people who have read the book and seen the movie may wonder about: Why was the tribe changed to the Sioux? Primarily it had to do with the location we ultimately chose.

It was really the buffalo that pointed us toward South Dakota. We had almost settled for another location, but I'd heard that there was a large herd on a ranch outside the capital of Pierre, South Dakota. We made contact with Roy Houck, a former lieutenant governor of the state, and flew out to his ranch, where he tends to the largest private herd of buffalo in the world . . . 3,500 head. And we knew that we'd found it. As Kevin says, it was like gold dust suddenly started to drop on the project.

South Dakota had the added benefit of one of the largest Native American communities in the country, the Sioux. We drew from numerous reservations, including the Rosebud, Pine Ridge, and Eagle Butte. Once they got a sense of what our movie was about, and the efforts we made to portray them realistically, they offered tremendous support and cooperation. People like Doris Leader Charge, who worked as our Lakota language translator/coach and plays Pretty Shield in the film, were at the heart of the project's success.

Casting the Native Americans was a challenge. We hired actors from all over the U.S. and Canada, and many tribes other than the Sioux participated (though 250 Sioux from the South Dakota reservations worked as extras). One criterion was that we had to have people with an authentic period look, and a lot of urban Indians had cut their hair, or didn't have the right look. But our casting director, Elizabeth Leustig, did an incredible job finding people who not only looked the part but brought the characters to life.

I didn't register the scope of this movie until we were actually on location and I added up how many period wagons we needed. (It was Kevin's wife, Cindy, who was finally thrown into action rounding up some forty wagons.) I hadn't quite imagined what Kevin had in mind. I soon found out. For our buffalo hunt we ended up with a helicopter, 10 pickup trucks, 24 bareback Indian riders, 150 extras, 20 wranglers to handle a herd of 3,500 real buffalo, 25 recreated buffalo, and 7 cameras. Logistically, what we managed to accomplish still amazes me, and there were plenty of people who doubted we could pull it off. They said it couldn't be done for the amount of money we had . . . that it was ridiculous for Kevin in his directorial debut to take on such a problematic period film involving children, animals, and the challenge of shooting in all four seasons.

How Kevin would handle his multiple roles was the biggest question prior to shooting. I'd worked with him before and knew he had incredible stamina—but the fact was that his character is present in all but a few scenes, while at the same time he's directing, seeing to production details, and doing most of his own stunts. This all had to go on for 108 grueling days of filming.

Kevin, Michael, and I identified closely with the character of Lieutenant John J. Dunbar and his desire to see the West while it was still intact. We all value independence in our lives and have sought out frontiers of our own.

The greatest satisfaction was in realizing what we set out to do. "Dances With Wolves" took us all on an incredible journey.

About this book: In creating a book about "Dances With Wolves," we wanted to give readers and viewers some idea of what went into making the movie. So in addition to telling the story and illustrating it with Ben Glass's photographs, we've described some of the work that went into costumes, sets, and props . . . how the actors learned to speak their lines in Lakota . . . how some of the difficult scenes were shot . . . how the Native Americans felt about taking part in this story.

Rather than publishing the entire screenplay, with its extensive staging directions, we have chosen to highlight key scenes and summarize some of the action in prose narrative. This is indicated typographically, with the screenplay excerpts printed in larger type. As is common practice in published screenplays, we have included certain scenes that ultimately were cut from the film released by Orion Pictures, and such scenes are marked with a symbol.

We hope that in showing some of the story behind the movie, this book reflects the spirit and care that went into making "Dances With Wolves."

Author's Notes

Like most children of the fifties, my first impressions of Native American people were not very positive. Indians were widely portrayed as devils, whose destruction was purely a matter of necessity in the process of taming the West. Every publication or film I saw as a child was slanted in this way.

But from the first, I sensed somehow that the story was incomplete. Late in elementary school I read a book by Quentin Reynolds that was written for young readers. I can't remember the title, but the book was about Custer and the Seventh Cavalry and the Little Big Horn. I enjoyed it immensely and, as most boys would, I identified strongly with the white soldiers.

There was something else, however, that sparked my interest for years to come. One particular Indian was portrayed in Reynolds' book as a great warrior and leader—Crazy Horse. From the moment I read about him I wanted to know more. Perhaps it was the ring of his name or the description of his fighting spirit, but I recall distinctly that I laid the book down with the thought, "I'd like to know more about that Crazy Horse."

In succeeding years I never fully lost the desire to know more, but it wasn't until my mid-twenties that I encountered the Indian people again, this time in reading Dee Brown's classic *Bury My Heart at Wounded Knee*. I was stunned, heartbroken, and enlightened.

But another ten years passed before I became fully involved. In my mid-thirties I reread *Bury My Heart*. . . . It was just as powerful the second time around and I found myself suddenly hungry for more of the Indian story. I started picking up other books. I read and read and read.

Another ten years have passed and I am still reading Native American history. It is often a sad study of genocide, of cultural annihilation perpetrated by our forefathers in the name of growth and of the "future generations" that we now comprise.

When I think of what was lost in the trampling of the great horse culture and its people, I am made immeasurably sad. Here were a people living in rough perfection; at home with sky, earth, and plain; strong families living in societies that valued and cared for their members. Not only was most of this destroyed but what little remained was locked up on reservations in desolate territory, far from public sight.

So the novel *Dances With Wolves* was written in part because I wanted to present some of the record of history as I see it. It was my hope that in showing what was lost, something might be regained—not the least of which could be new respect for the proud descendants of the people I wrote about, who are living yet on reserves where our ancestors confined them.

Everything was so unspoiled in 1863—the year *Dances With Wolves* takes place—but I missed it all. And by reading history I could imagine it only to a point. By creating Lieutenant Dunbar, I could actually live it to an extent that surpassed my expectations. I am living it still.

But I think love is probably the biggest reason for the existence of *Dances With Wolves*. I love the animals with whom we share the planet. I love the humbling quality of open space. I love the West as it once was, teeming with buffalo and wolves. And I love the reverent, free people from whom I have learned so much.

I am blessed now with the opportunity to share the love I feel. The novel is being reissued, an unabridged audio version of the book has been produced, a masterful film of the story has been mounted, and, for those who want to know more, there is this beautiful and informative volume from Newmarket Press.

To be able to share this great bounty of storytelling with so many is a writer's dream come true.

The strangeness of this life cannot be measured...

Lt. John Dunbar

The Killing Field

St. David's Field, Tennessee, 1863

As the Union Army advanced through Tennessee in the bloody autumn of 1863, two small units of Federal and Confederate troops faced each other across two hundred yards of open field. The stalemate had been going on for three days, neither side sure of the other's strength, neither willing to make a decisive move. But deadly sniper fire took its toll on men from both sides.

In the Union field hospital tent lay a young lieutenant named John J. Dunbar, with a deep shrapnel wound in his leg that reached to the bone. He listened through a fog of pain as two exhausted Army surgeons marked him down for an amputation—just another of many they had performed that day—as soon as they got back from a coffee break.

Dunbar sat up painfully on his cot, found a discarded boot from an earlier amputee and a cane to clench between his teeth. He almost fainted as he pulled the boot on, but managed to sneak out of the tent and limp back to his outfit without anyone noticing him.

There he found his comrades disgusted and demoralized by their inaction and the indecisiveness of the field officers leading them. Both they and their enemies crouched behind low stone walls at opposite ends of the field, waiting for . . . they knew not what. Neither did the major in command, all the more unsettled because his master, General Tide, had arrived to observe the action.

Gesturing toward the trees behind them, where several men were clustered around a huge hunk of material attached to a gondola, Sergeant Pepper brought Dunbar up to date:

PEPPER

We started a balloon up but they shot her down 'fore she was ten feet off the ground . . . so nobody's made a run either way. It's been a standoff all damn day . . . and now the major, he's lookin' at the general and he's thinkin' I better do somethin', and you know what that means. . . .

But Dunbar was no longer listening. He was scanning the row of picketed horses, a strange idea taking shape in his mind through the insistent pain. He was going to die anyway, or so the doctors had said. . . . All right, at least he'd die with both feet on. And maybe he could do something worthy of a soldier before he died, something he'd be remembered for.

Without a word to anyone, he stumbled toward the line of horses, heading for a compactly built buckskin he'd noticed. Hauling himself into the saddle, he spurred his mount toward the stone wall, the horse rising to clear it over the head of a startled Sergeant Pepper.

As they sped toward the Confederate line, soldiers on both sides of the field roused from their torpor and stared in amazement . . . the rebels scrambling to load their rifles. On the hill above the valley, General Tide peered through his pocket telescope and shook his head in wonder. It looked like suicide.

[Battlefield]

Dunbar can see the Confederate riflemen now. They're rising up behind the wall to aim and fire.

Fifty yards from the enemy line, he's still unhit.

He wheels the buckskin into a sharp left turn and they

streak parallel to the Confederate flank . . . The firing is
tremendous. The lieutenant's hat is torn away, and a slug
lifts one of his epaulets, but still no bullet finds him.

The lieutenant pulls the buckskin up at the far end
of the field. He bows his head in exhaustion, but a sound
coming across the field brings his head up quickly. A great
cheer is rolling along the Union line. . . .

Dunbar gazes down along his leg. Blood is pumping
from his wound. Again he digs his heels into the buckskin's
flanks and they fly down the line. The Confederates are

trying to reload. A few are able to get off a hasty shot, but they're all too late.

Dunbar swerves a little closer to the wall as he approaches the other half of the Confederate ranks. The lieutenant shuts his eyes, lets the reins flop on the buckskin's neck, and spreads his arms as they thunder toward the line of riflemen.

General Tide charged down the hill with his aides behind him and leaped the wall. The Union troops followed him as one man, in full-throated battle cry as they poured across the field. The rebels broke and scattered toward the woods.

[Battlefield]
Suddenly the field is quiet. There is rifle fire in the distance, but otherwise everything is still. At one end of the field is a solitary buckskin horse. His rider lies on the ground, a foot hooked in one stirrup.

The sound of men's voices is coming near. Suddenly, General Tide is peering down at him. Dunbar stares back, glassy-eyed.

DUNBAR
Don't take off my foot.

General Tide stares down into Dunbar's blank face. He kneels next to the lieutenant and bends to whisper in his ear.

GENERAL TIDE
You rest easy, son . . . you'll keep your foot. As God is my judge, you'll keep it.

The general looks up at one of his aides.

GENERAL TIDE

Bring up my ambulance. And bring my surgeon
with it. We've got an officer who's worth something
lying here.

The general found himself deeply moved by Dunbar's sacrifice. True
to his word, he arranged for his own surgeon to salvage the lieutenant's
foot, and followed his recovery closely. Believing that Dunbar had made
more than his just contribution to Civil War combat, he offered him
any post of his choosing away from the front lines.

Dunbar's answer came as a surprise to all but himself. He asked to be
posted West, on the frontier. It didn't matter where, but it was his long-
held dream to see the vast expanses of prairie and sky about which he'd
heard so much. Now, having been reborn in a way, he was ready for a
new life.

His only other request was to keep the buckskin horse.

The country is everything I
dreamed it would be. There can
be no place like this on earth.

PART 1

The Frontier

Fort Hays, Dakota Territory

DUNBAR'S JOURNAL

"The strangeness of this life cannot be measured. In trying to produce my own death, I was elevated to the status of a living hero."

In the spring, Lieutenant John Dunbar made the long and weary journey westward. With the sturdy buckskin—now named Cisco—that had carried him safely through the Confederate fire in Tennessee, he took a steamer up the Missouri to Fort Pierre. Then they set out across country for Fort Hays, the last good-sized garrison in the Dakota plains.

The country west of the Cheyenne River was the ancestral domain of the Lakota Sioux, but other tribes, such as the Crow and the fierce Pawnee, also roamed and raided there. The troops at Fort Hays had not engaged in any large-scale Indian fighting in this region . . . that would come later, when greater matters back East were settled.

For the most part, they were ignored—both by the Indians and by their masters in the East. As long as they rode out in fair-sized patrols, the Indians avoided them. Small groups of travelers and homesteaders, though, were vulnerable if certain Indians decided they were trespassing.

Dunbar was deeply excited by his first glimpse of the prairie as he and Cisco rode out to the fort. In a way he could not have explained, he felt as if he were coming home.

His orders were to report to a Major Fambrough, the fort's commander. He found Fambrough in his office, and the encounter was a strange one. Though Dunbar had no way of knowing it, the major's years of isolation at the post, of failing to advance in his military career, of alcoholic and lonely bachelorhood, had taken a massive toll on his unstable personality. He was delusional and quietly deranged.

[Fambrough's office]

> **FAMBROUGH**
> *(indicating paper)* Your orders say you are to be posted on the frontier. The frontier is Indian country. I quickly deduced that you are an Indian fighter.

He arches an eyebrow, challenging the lieutenant. He has sad swollen eyes. He is an Army lifer passed over too many times for promotion, and right now does not look like a well man.

> **FAMBROUGH**
> I did not ascend to this position by being stupid.

> **DUNBAR**
> No, sir.

Dunbar watches Fambrough in silence. The major's tunic is covered with food stains. Sweat has broken out all over his head. His grooming is awful. His hands are trembling slightly. Something is very wrong with him.

Now the major sees something on the official paper. He looks quickly at the lieutenant, then back at the paper, moving his lips but making no sound.

FAMBROUGII

It says here you've been decorated. And they sent
you out here to be posted?

DUNBAR

Actually, sir, I'm here at my own request . . . I want
to see the frontier . . . before it's gone.

The major fixes Dunbar with a sly look.

FAMBROUGH

Such a smart lad, coming straight to me.

Still sly, Fambrough digs into a side drawer. There is
the distinct clink of glass on glass as he rummages. Now
Fambrough has what he wants, a blank official form. He
begins to fill it out, writing in a disturbingly childish way.

FAMBROUGII

Sir Knight, I am sending you on a knight's
errand. You will report to Captain Cargill at
the furthermost outpost of the realm . . .
Fort Sedgewick.

He looks over his work with a schoolboy's excitement and
affixes his signature with a wild flourish.

FAMBROUGH

My personal seal will assure you safe passage
through many miles of wild, hostile country.

He folds the order and hands it to Dunbar.

DUNBAR

I'm wondering, sir, how will I be getting there?

FAMBROUGH
You think I don't know?

DUNBAR
No, sir . . . it's just that I don't know.

FAMBROUGH
Hold your tongue.

The major turns in his chair to stare through a single, dusty window. He can see a teamster outside, tying down canvas on a heavily loaded wagon.

FAMBROUGH
I'm in a generous mood and will grant your boon.
You see that peasant . . . he calls himself
Timmons. He leaves this very afternoon for your
Fort Sedgewick. Ride with him if you like . . . he
knows the way. That is all.

Dunbar salutes and Fambrough returns it mockingly. The lieutenant starts for the door.

FAMBROUGH
Sir Knight . . .

Dunbar turns around. Fambrough is standing in front of his desk. There's a large, dark splotch on the major's trouser front. He jams both hands into the front of his pants and giggles.

FAMBROUGH
I just pissed my pants . . . and nobody can do
anything about it.

The interview with Major Fambrough made Dunbar's skin crawl, and he was anxious to be away from there. He hastily found the teamster's wagon and arranged passage to his new destination, Fort Sedgewick. As the wagon rumbled out of Fort Hays, Dunbar heard a solitary gunshot behind them. He had no way of knowing that it was Fambrough's own pistol, ending the unhappy major's life. Now not a soul except the wagon driver, Timmons, knew where Lieutenant John Dunbar was going.

DUNBAR'S JOURNAL
"We have been gone four days now, and still we have seen no signs of life. Only earth and sky."

The journey from Fort Hays to Fort Sedgewick was 150 miles or so, and for Dunbar it could have gone on forever. He had fallen in love with the prairie. Its wide-open horizons both thrilled and soothed him; something in his spirit responded to this place like no other. At night he sat by the fire writing in his journal and marveling at the enormous, star-filled sky, where shooting stars would now and then streak across the heavens.

He looked forward to seeing Indians for the first time with a mixture of excitement and dread. On the third day out, they came upon the burnt-out remains of a wagon and a cluster of bleached bones in the grass. Finding an arrow through a human skeleton, Dunbar could only guess at the drama that had been played out here.

It would have been paradise except for the presence of the crude, foul-smelling Timmons. When the wind was wrong, Dunbar couldn't even bear to sit next to him on the wagon seat, but would retreat to a perch on the mound of provisions at the rear of the wagon. Sometimes he untied Cisco from the stern and rode off through the rolling ocean of grass to scout from a rise. But he never saw anything but small animals and the occasional antelope or hawk.

> *"Were it not for my companion, I believe I would be having the time of my life. I know he means well but he is quite possibly the foulest person I have ever met."*

*Unbeknownst to Dunbar or Timmons, a ragged column of soldiers was moving slowly across the prairie some miles away, making the same journey but in the opposite direction.

The tiny garrison at Fort Sedgewick had waited in vain for supplies and fresh troops for many months. But the war in the East had stretched the Army's resources too thin, and remote frontier outposts came last on everyone's list.

Some men had deserted. All but two scrawny horses were lost to Indian raids. The remaining handful of soldiers, malnourished and mutinous, had scratched out caves in the cliffside below the fort, where they huddled for protection. Finally their commander, Captain Cargill, assembled his ragtag company and told them it was over—he was taking them back to Fort Hays and taking responsibility for the consequences.

[Prairie]

Near the end of the journey, on the tenth day, Dunbar is walking through a little valley of tall, rich grass. The wagon is nowhere in sight. He looks fondly back at Cisco, who is also wandering by himself searching for prime shoots.

Timmons' wagon comes into view now.

DUNBAR'S JOURNAL

> *"Despite our late starts we have explored much of this great country. It would seem to be endless. For all of Timmons' chatter he cannot say when we will arrive at Fort Sedgewick.*

*Reader's note: This scene was one of several cut from the final film due to length. The beginning and end of such scenes are marked with this symbol I.I.

There is still no sign of human life save the bones we passed some five days ago. I am certain I have made the right choice and I am anxious to see my new home."

DUNBAR

How come we haven't seen any buffalo?

TIMMONS

Can't figger the stinkin' buffalo. Sometimes you don't see 'em for days, sometimes they're thick as curls on a whore.

DUNBAR

What about Indians?

TIMMONS

Goddamn Indians you'd jus' as soon not see, lessen the bastards are dead. Nothing but thieves and beggars.

The wagon disappears over the ridge, and again Dunbar is alone. In gentle awe, he runs his palm over the top of the grass swirling about his waist. He scans the horizon in all directions, aware all at once of his aloneness. He flips the reins over Cisco's neck and sticks a foot in the stirrup.

As Dunbar comes over the hill, he sees that the wagon has ground to a stop at the edge of a bluff. Dunbar and Timmons peer into the little valley below.

TIMMONS

Not what you'd call a going concern.

The wagon lurches over the top of the bluff and down. We see the pathetic remains of Fort Sedgewick.

The scene shifts to a full view of the deserted fort. Timmons sits on the wagon by himself.

TIMMONS
Ain't nothin' here, lieutenant.

Dunbar appears from Cargill's former quarters.

TIMMONS (OS)
Everybody's run off . . . or got kilt.

The lieutenant looks briefly at Timmons and marches over to the caved-in supply house. Again he ducks inside. Then he emerges from the supply house and stares up at the wagon driver.

DUNBAR
All right . . . let's unload the wagon.

TIMMONS
What, and leave it all here?

DUNBAR
I'm staying too . . . we don't know what's happened.

Dunbar moves around to the back of the wagon.

TIMMONS
There ain't nothin' here, lieutenant.

DUNBAR
Not at the moment, no.

TIMMONS
So things bein' the way they are, we might as well turn around and get started back.

DUNBAR

This is my post . . .

TIMMONS

This is my post . . . are you crazy, boy?

The lieutenant's eyes have gone absolutely black. Suddenly the long revolver holstered at his hip is in his hand and pointing at Timmons' head.

DUNBAR

This is my post! And those are the post's provisions. Now get your ass off that wagon and help me unload.

Timmons scrambled to obey, and soon the supplies were stacked in the yard. Dunbar retrieved a case of eggs from the pile and handed them up to Timmons as the driver prepared to depart. Timmons wished the lieutenant luck and promised to let the Army know where he was. Then he clucked to his mules and the wagon rumbled off, disappearing over the bluff.

DUNBAR'S JOURNAL

"Have arrived to find Fort Sedgewick deserted. Am now waiting for the garrison's return or word from headquarters. Post is in exceedingly poor condition. Have decided to assign myself clean-up duty beginning tomorrow. Supplies abundant.

"The country is everything I dreamed it would be. There can be no place like this on earth."

Dunbar set to his task the next day, and it occupied him for several more. He hammered nails into the broken-down corral and policed up his quarters and the supply hut. Soon both were stacked to the rafters with the provisions from Fort Hays. He also discovered the rough caves hollowed into the cliff and filled them in, puzzling over the deepening mystery of the fort and its missing men.

As the bottom of the slope below the fort was a squalid dump where the ill-fated garrison threw their refuse, choking the banks of the stream that flowed there. Worst of all, the stream and watering hole were full of an assortment of rotting carcasses killed by the starving men for food. One by one, Dunbar laboriously hauled them out of the water and up the bank—with help from Cisco, rigged in a makeshift harness.

When the last corpse had been heaved onto the huge pile, he soaked it with fuel oil and lighted the pyre. As a towering column of black smoke rose into the sky, he realized in belated horror that he'd just sent an obvious signal to any Indians for miles around.

No Indians appeared to investigate Dunbar's blaze . . . but another fire a few dozen miles away was attracting the attention of a small Indian party: four warriors, two injured men on travois, and their ponies.

[Prairie]
They are Pawnee, the scariest of all the Plains tribes. One man a little apart looks The Toughest. The four men are squatting on their haunches, staring in the same direction from a low rise on the prairie.

It's smoke, a column much smaller than Dunbar's, drifting up from a distant line of rolling gullies.

THE TOUGHEST
Only a white man would make a fire for everyone to see.

1ST PAWNEE
Maybe there's more than one.

The Toughest turns back to face the others. Without another word, he jumps on his horse. Another silence as the other three warriors consider what to do.

2ND PAWNEE
We have no rifles. White men are sure to have rifles.

3RD PAWNEE
We should forget this and go home.

The Toughest has listened all the while, growing more and more disgusted. He pulls the blanket from his shoulders and flings it angrily at his companions.

THE TOUGHEST
Then go. I, for one, will not debate the merit of a single line of smoke in my own country.

He starts his pony walking down the rise toward the smoke.

1ST PAWNEE
(shaking his head) He will not quit until we are all dead.

When the Pawnee investigated, they discovered that the source of the smoke was the wagoneer Timmons, on his way back to Fort Hays and unwise enough to build his supper fire with green wood. Taking their time—he was only one man, after all—they slaughtered him with arrow after arrow, and then rode off with his scalp and whatever gear they did not disdain.

Back at Fort Sedgewick, Dunbar was unaware that the last man on earth who knew of his whereabouts was dead. He did know that he was still at a loss for what to do about his situation.

"No sign of Captain Cargill's command. I don't know what to do. Communication can only take place if I leave, and I don't want to abandon my post. Made a short patrol yesterday p.m. . . . discovered nothing. Will go further tomorrow."

While working at his chores one afternoon, Dunbar looked up and was startled to see a lone wolf sitting in the grass not a hundred yards away, watching him. His first instinct was to reach for his gun—but

something stopped him. It wasn't as if he needed to hunt for food, and the animal seemed more curious than dangerous.

From then on, the wolf reappeared almost every day. Dunbar, for lack of other entertainment, began trying to coax the creature nearer, enticing it with scraps of dried meat.

DUNBAR'S JOURNAL

"There is a wolf who seems intent on the goings-on here. He does not seem inclined to be a nuisance, however, and aside from Cisco has been my only company. He has appeared each afternoon for the past two days. He has milky white socks on both front feet. If he comes calling tomorrow, I will name him Two Socks."

And for many days after that, Cisco and Two Socks remained his only company.

Tomorrow morning I will ride
out to the Indians. I do not know
the outcome or the wisdom of this . . .

PART II

The Real Natural Human Beings

Fort Sedgewick, Dakota Territory

DUNBAR'S JOURNAL

"Almost a month and no one has come. The longer this condition persists, the less inclined I am to believe that anyone will. Rain has forced me indoors for most of two days. I have begun an awning. The work has ruined my hands, but I am excited about the improvement it will bring to this place. It is the loneliest of times . . . but I cannot say that I am unhappy."

Dunbar's solitude was about to be broken. One morning he was down at the riverbank washing his clothes. Squatting naked at the edge of the stream, he pounded the dirt out of his trousers on a little rock ledge.

Over the rise, out of his line of vision, someone was standing in the tall prairie grass, gazing thoughtfully at the "new" Fort Sedgewick: the tidy grounds, the great awning, the repaired corral. The beautiful buckskin inside it.

It was a lone Indian, his pony at his side. His spectacular face radiated wisdom. He was a person of special maturity and responsibility in his community, a Sioux medicine man named Kicking Bird.

[Riverbank]
Comfortable with his nakedness, Dunbar is meandering along the stream in no particular hurry. He's very white. His skin practically sparkles in the sun.

Dunbar is making his way up the bluff. The steepest part is at the lip, and here he drops to all fours. His face comes into view, and he freezes.

Someone is creeping under the shade of the awning . . . an aboriginal man.

Dunbar's head pops down behind the bluff. He is down on his naked haunches, his heart pounding in his ears. Sweat has broken out on his face. His mouth is dry as ash. He's playing back images in fragments: A deerskin shirt, strands of hair sewn along each sleeve. Fringed leggings. A dark, faded breechclout. Moccasins with beading. A single, large feather drooping behind a head of shiny black hair. Braids wrapped in fur. A lethal stone club hanging from a red hand. No eyebrows on a magnificent, primitive face.

Dunbar stays in a crouch, trying to think on jellied legs. His breathing has quickened. His mouth is open.

A horse's whinny startles him. Ever so slowly, the lieutenant peers over the bluff.

The aboriginal man is in the corral. He's walking slowly toward Cisco. One hand is held out reassuringly, the other is grasping a rope. He's making gentle, cooing sounds and is only a step or two from being able to loop his line over the horse's neck.

DUNBAR
You there!

Kicking Bird jumps straight into the air. As he lands, he whirls to meet the voice that startled him.

Dunbar is coming. His hands are clenched and his arms are swinging stiffly at his sides.

Kicking Bird has turned to stone at the sight of this horror. With a sharp intake of breath, he staggers back a few steps. Then he turns and runs, tearing through the corral fence as if it were made of twigs. He leaps onto his horse and quirts the pony into a full gallop.

Dunbar is watching from the yard. His jaw is clenched, his hands are still fisted. But the great grassland is empty. Kicking Bird is gone.

DUNBAR'S JOURNAL

"Have made first contact with a wild Indian. One came to the fort and tried to steal my horse. Do not know how many more are in the vicinity, but I am taking steps for another visitation. Am burying excess ordance, lest it fall into enemy hands."

Besides burying the guns and ammunition, Dunbar cached most of his provisions, carved a window out of the wall of his sod hut to sight through, and pared down his afternoon rides to short patrols around the fort.

DUNBAR'S JOURNAL

"Have made all the preparations I can think of. I cannot mount an adequate defense, but will try to make a big impression when they come. Waiting.

"The man I encountered was a magnificent-looking fellow."

The Sioux of the Ten Bears band, about 150 strong, had just returned to their ancestral summer hunting camp some twelve miles west of Fort Sedgewick. The medicine man, Kicking Bird, had ridden out on his own to get away from the clamor of the resettlement, to see how the prairie was doing this year and feel the presence of the Great Spirit calm his heart.

But after finding the naked *wasichu* (white man) so unexpectedly at the fort they had assumed was dead, his heart did not feel peaceful at all. His people hadn't had much trouble with whites so far, but he had heard that many more of them were coming. Soldiers always came in numbers, though—why was there just this one at the soldier fort? Was there something special about him?

Ten Bears, the band's venerable leader, noticed that Kicking Bird was not himself. After a day or so, he decided to give his friend a chance to talk about whatever was bothering him.

I⁺I   *[Kicking Bird's lodge]*
Kicking Bird sits in his lodge next to the fire, playing with his son—but he is preoccupied with something. There is a rustle of movement at the tent flap, and Ten Bears peers in.

TEN BEARS
May I come in?

The little boy races over to the old chief. Kicking Bird makes a move to pull him back, but Ten Bears indicates the boy should stay.

TEN BEARS
No, no, let him sit with me.

There is silence as the two men settle themselves by the fire, the little boy content in Ten Bears' lap.

TEN BEARS
Our country seems good this summer, but I have not been out to see it.

KICKING BIRD
Yes . . . it is good. The grass is rich. The game is plenty and not running away.

TEN BEARS
I am glad to hear it. But the buffalo are late. I always worry about the bellies of our children.

A brief silence.

KICKING BIRD
I was thinking of a dance.

TEN BEARS
Yes, a dance is always a good idea. It would be good to have a strong sign.

Kicking Bird seems suddenly uncomfortable. The little boy leaves.

TEN BEARS

There's a funny thing about signs. They are always flying in our faces. We know when they are bad or good but sometimes they are strange and there is no way to understand them. Sometimes they make people crazy but a smart man will take such a sign into himself and let it run around for two or three days. If he is still confused he will tell somebody. He might come to you or to me and tell it. A smart man always does that.

Kicking Bird opens up and tells the old chief what he has seen. Ten Bears decides that a council is in order.

[Ten Bears' lodge]

The eldest and most respected men of the band, including Ten Bears and his pal Stone Calf, an influential warrior named Wind In His Hair, and Kicking Bird are seated around the fire. Crowded around them, in a high state of excitement, are the village's leading warriors. The meeting is in progress.

KICKING BIRD

He might be a god or he might be a special chief—that's why we are thinking of having a talk with him.

There is a little murmuring around the fire, and it goes silent. Wind In His Hair rises to speak.

WIND IN HIS HAIR

I do not care for this talk about a white man. Whatever kind of white man he is, he is not a Sioux

and that makes him less. We've camped here for ten days now and each day our scouts find nothing. We need meat—not talk.

KICKING BIRD
You are right, we need meat today and tomorrow. But we must also have meat in ten years.

Kicking Bird pauses here. Everyone is listening attentively.

KICKING BIRD

But the whites are coming. Our friends the Shoshone and the Kiowa, even our enemies, agree on this—the whites are coming. More than can be counted.

WIND IN HIS HAIR

Kicking Bird is always looking ahead, and that is good. But when I hear that more whites are coming, more than can be counted, I want to laugh. We took a hundred horses from these people, there was no honor in it. They don't ride well, they don't shoot well, they're dirty. They have no women, no children. They could not even make it through one winter in our country. And these people are said to flourish? I think they will all be dead in ten years.

There is a surge of enthusiasm in the lodge, and Wind In His Hair is riding the crest of it.

WIND IN HIS HAIR

I think this white man is probably lost.

This parting shot prompts a good-natured round of laughter.

KICKING BIRD

Wind In His Hair has spoken straight. His words are strong and I have heard them. It's true that the whites are a poor race, and it's hard to understand them. But when I see one white man alone, without fear in our country, I do not think he is lost. I think he may have medicine. I see someone who might speak for all the white people who are coming. I think this is a person with whom treaties might be struck.

WIND IN HIS HAIR
This white man cannot cover our lodges, or string our bows, or feed our children. I will take some good men . . . there are many here tonight. We will ride to the soldier fort, we will shoot some arrows into this white man. If he truly has medicine, he will not be hurt. If he has no medicine, he will be dead.

This is the best idea so far and there is much talk around the fire. They quiet down as Ten Bears prepares to speak.

STONE CALF
No man can tell another what to do. But killing a white man is a delicate matter. If you kill one, more are sure to come.

Ten Bears nods, and they all wait for his response.

TEN BEARS
It is easy to become confused by these questions. It is hard to know what to do. We should talk about this some more. That is all I have to say.

He drops his head, closes his eyes, and starts to fall asleep. The meeting is over.

A Sioux teenager, Smiles A Lot, and his friends Otter and Worm eavesdropped on the council from outside the lodge, and hatched a plot

to ride to Fort Sedgewick in the middle of the night and steal Cisco from the "white god." Such a feat would earn them considerable prestige.

They managed to make off with the horse, as Dunbar knocked himself unconscious in the doorway while charging outside in response to Cisco's whinny. But Cisco had other ideas. He bolted away from the youngsters leading him back to the village, yanking Otter off his pony and breaking his arm.

Dunbar was relieved to have Cisco back—there was a strong bond between them. But the night raid only added to his edginess. He had no doubt the Indians would come again.

After the boys came back from their unsuccessful raid, Wind In His Hair could no longer restrain himself from riding to the white soldier's camp. He would take a small party of men—not boys—and do no shooting unless the white man shot first. But he would prove that no magic protected the fort. Since in Sioux society, any respected warrior could ultimately do whatever he wanted, no one tried to stop Wind In His Hair.

[Riverbank]
Dunbar is shaving in the shallow river below the fort. The big Navy revolver and his gunbelt are slung over his shoulder. Dunbar glances at the far bluff, where Two Socks is sitting quietly, watching the shaving ritual below.

As he finishes shaving his moustache, the lieutenant glances up at Two Socks again. The wolf's attention has been diverted. He's on guard, staring intently across the river.

Dunbar looks quickly at the bluff nearest the fort. Everything is still. He looks back at Two Socks. The wolf is gone.

The lieutenant hears something now. Hoofbeats. Hoofbeats coming in a rush. He bursts from the water and scrambles up the incline.

They're streaming past him. Six mounted warriors bunched around Cisco: raw, powerful men on painted, feathered ponies. Wind In His Hair is one of them. Their faces are streaked with colorful designs, their weapons slung around the shoulders, their nearly naked bodies all sinew and bone. They are the full and breathtaking glory of war.

Dunbar is struck dumb. He stands still as the pageant passes in front of him.

The sight of Dunbar troubles Wind In His Hair so much that he pulls up a hundred yards away. He sits a moment on his whirling pony, trying to decide if he should confront the white god. He makes a warrior's choice. Wind

In His Hair shouts to his fellows to go on and charges down the slope . . . straight for Dunbar.

Dunbar's eyes are fixed on the closing horseman. He can't move.

Wind In His Hair is coming flat out, his lance extended. At the last moment, he pulls up so hard that the black pony skids to a sit. The horse is up quickly and hard to manage. He pitches back and forth only a few feet in front of Lieutenant Dunbar.

WIND IN HIS HAIR
I am Wind In His Hair. Do you not see that I am not afraid of you? . . . Do you see?

Dunbar stares expressionlessly into the Sioux's eyes. He doesn't blink.

Wind In His Hair suddenly turns his pony and whips after his comrades. A big smile breaks out across his face.

Dunbar stares after the disappearing horse and rider. He feels the weight of the gun and lets it drop to the ground. He takes a few steps back toward his quarters, then crumples to the ground in a dead faint.

But Cisco once again broke free of his captors on the journey back to the village, and not even six superb horsemen could catch Dunbar's extraordinarily fast and agile mount in full flight. Rather than run their ponies into the ground, they turned back, marveling at the white man's good fortune in owning such an animal—perhaps he really did have some magic. Wind In His Hair was equally impressed with the lieutenant's coolness in the face of his threatening charge.

Arriving back in the village, Wind In His Hair and the others learned that a party that had been away fighting the Pawnee had fared badly. Several good warriors had been lost, and there was great sorrow.

One young widow was especially devastated by grief. She had the manner and bearing of a Sioux, but there was something different about her. If one looked closely at her dark, cherry colored hair, sharp features, and light brown eyes, it was clear that she was white—or once had been. Stands With A Fist had been with the tribe since early childhood, however, discovered alone on the prairie by the Sioux after her family was massacred by Pawnee. Ten Bears' band was the only family she remembered.

And she had been very much in love with her warrior husband. After an initial outburst of hysterical grief, she resolved to mourn him in the traditional way. She went out of the village to a place where she could be alone, to think about him and their life together, to sing his praise, to shed some of her own blood in memory of his death. For this purpose she took with her a sharp knife.

Dunbar's latest encounter with the Indians aroused him from the waiting mode he had been in.

DUNBAR'S JOURNAL

"I realize now that I have been wrong. All this time I have been waiting. . . . Waiting for what? For Indians to steal my horse? To see a buffalo? Since I arrived at this post, I have been walking on eggs. It has become a bad habit and I am sick of it.

"Tomorrow morning I will ride out to the Indians. I do not know the outcome or the wisdom of this thinking. But I have become a target, and a target makes a poor impression. I am through waiting."

Determined to make the best impression he was capable of, Dunbar polished his boots and buttons, brushed his uniform and Cisco's coat.

TWO SOCKS

There is a wolf who seems intent on the gorge out here. He does not seem inclined to be a nuisance however and aside from Cisco has been my only company. He has appeared each afternoon for the past two days.

He has milky white socks on both feet.

If he comes calling tomorrow I will name him Two Socks.

Lt. John J. Dunbar

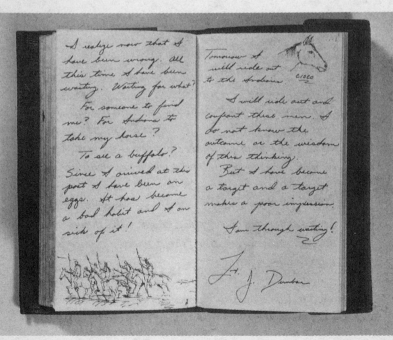

I realize now that I have been wrong. All this time I have been waiting. Waiting for what?

For someone to find me? For Indians to take my horse?

To see a buffalo? Since I arrived at this post I have been on edge. It has become a bad habit and I am sick of it!

Tomorrow I will ride out to the Indians

CISCO

I will ride out and confront these men. I do not know the outcome or the wisdom of this thinking.

But I have become a target and a target makes a poor impression.

I am through waiting!

Lt. J. Dunbar

He set off the next morning in the direction his visitors had taken, and where he'd been seeing smoke on the western horizon. Old Glory fluttered from a staff stuck into one of his boots.

After riding deep into the prairie for several miles, Dunbar's attention was caught by a strange, intermittent sound. Not a bird, he thought, riding closer, it sounded more like a weird kind of singing. Reaching the top of a knoll, he saw a figure seated by a solitary cottonwood tree.

Moving closer still, he saw that it was an Indian woman with knife in her hand and when she saw him and rose in alarm, the front of her dress was covered with blood. In making the small cuts in her flesh that were part of the mourning ritual, Stands With A Fist had cut her thigh too deeply and was bleeding from an arterial wound.

Dunbar, recovering from his shock, tried to approach her. But she was terrified of him. Her worst fear was that whites would come one day and take her away from her people.

[Prairie knoll]
She's too weak to run and falls face first in the grass. She starts to crawl.

Dunbar slips off Cisco and reaches down tentatively for her shoulder. She screams at his touch and he pulls away. But he follows her on foot as she crawls.

DUNBAR
You're hurt . . . you need help.

He takes her again, this time holding her firmly. She struggles mightily, twisting onto her back. She lashes out at his face but he grabs her hands, holding them tight. They're nose to nose.

STANDS WITH A FIST
(in English) Don't . . .

He can't believe he heard it, and she can't believe she said it. She spits out a stream of Sioux curses, throws her head back and wails like a wolf. Then she passes out.

Dunbar bound up Stands With A Fist's wounds as best he could, using strips torn from his flag. He couldn't help noticing that her skin under the dress was whiter than her exposed limbs and face, and he noted her reddish hair. Then the English word she had spoken . . . could she really be white?

But this was no time for speculation. Her pony was nearby, but it was clear she couldn't ride by herself, so he lifted her onto Cisco's back, mounted up behind, and continued riding slowly toward the village.

Just before reaching it, they passed through the pony herd, the size of which amazed him. Even more amazing was his first sight of Ten Bears' village spread out on the river's edge—the smoke from its many fires, the conical houses covered with well-used hides, the willow poles fanning against the sky, men, women, and children going about their tasks. It was a like a curtain rising on an ancient tableau, fully alive before his eyes.

Their first sight of him produced pandemonium. Moments after the alarm was raised, the entire village stood near the entrance facing him, warriors at the front. Wind In His Hair came forward, and when he realized it was Stands With A Fist whom Dunbar held, tore the woman from his arms and barked an order for him to leave.

Though he didn't understand the words, Dunbar got the message and rode slowly away, puzzled and disappointed. Several warriors wanted to ride after him, but Kicking Bird held them back, pointing

out that the white soldier clearly had not come to fight. But though he reached Fort Sedgewick safely, Dunbar felt his mission had been a failure.

[Ten Bears' lodge]
That night, another council is in progress. As before, the leading men are seated around Ten Bears' fire while the other warriors stand packed in the shadows. Wind In His Hair is seated close to the elders.

TEN BEARS
I am in agreement with Kicking Bird. We will go down and talk to the white man and find out what kind of white man he is.

Wind In His Hair jumps into the conversation.

WIND IN HIS HAIR
If this council decides to talk with the white man at

the soldier fort, then it will be so. But in my mind it is not right that a Sioux chief, a chief as great as Ten Bears, goes to ask the business of a puny, trespassing white man . . . a white soldier who has only a smart horse and a few white man's clothes.

There are many yeses in response to this. As is his custom, Ten Bears lets the outburst subside, seemingly unruffled. Casually, he pops a piece of meat into his mouth and begins to chew.

TEN BEARS
I will not go. You will go . . . you and Kicking Bird. That is all I have to say.

The next day, eight Sioux warriors appeared on the bluff above Fort Sedgewick. Six stayed there while the other two rode slowly down toward the fort. Dunbar reached for his rifle as they started, then thought better of it and went out to meet them.

He made them as welcome as he could and hoped they took his meaning. Kicking Bird made the Sioux sign of greeting, and the two Indians looked around the fort with great curiosity. They and Dunbar had no success in understanding each other, however, until the lieutenant decided to ask about the buffalo, whose absence puzzled him as much as it did the Sioux.

He performed a crude imitation of the animal, with a blanket wadded under his shirt for a hump, fingers pointing from his head as horns, snorting and bellowing. Wind In His Hair thought he was simply mad, but Kicking Bird caught on and offered the Sioux word for "buffalo." Dunbar eagerly imitated it until he got it right. It was a beginning.

*"The Fierce One, as I call him, seems a very tough fellow.
I hope I never have to fight him. From what little I know
so far, he seems an honest and perfectly direct fellow.*

*"I like the Quiet One immensely. He has been patient
and inquisitive. He seems eager to communicate. I
would conclude that he is a man of some weight among
his people."*

The visits of Kicking Bird and Wind In His Hair continued. One
day Dunbar entertained them by grinding coffee beans in a strange
machine, then offered them fresh coffee. The taste didn't impress them
at first . . . until he supplied sugar to go with it. He began to learn
a little sign language, and felt encouraged about the possibilities
for communication.

*"So much goes unsaid, though, and I have the curious
feeling that these people, the Quiet One in particular, want
something from me. What it is I cannot guess. But I don't
believe I go too far in saying that a foundation for good
relations is being laid."*

At night, Dunbar described the strange meetings in his journal and
sketched the likenesses of his Indian neighbors. He also practiced the
hand signals.

*"So far I have learned the words for head, hand, horse,
fire, coffee, buffalo, hello and goodbye. But it is not nearly
enough. The Quiet One seems as eager for barriers to be*

broken as I am. For some odd reason, he insists on calling
me Loo Ten Tant. I have tried to break him of this but he
persists. I have to admit . . . it does have a distinctive ring."

Kicking Bird was indeed growing impatient with the slow pace of
communication. He decided to use a resource he had not called on
before. He and his wife had taken Stands With A Fist into their lodge
while she recovered. If the girl could be persuaded to remember the
language she had spoken as a child, he could speak to Loo Ten Tant
through her. When he judged her physical and emotional wounds
sufficiently healed, he called her into his lodge to talk.

[Kicking Bird's lodge]
They seat themselves at the firepit in the center of the lodge.
A brief silence, during which Kicking Bird studies the girl
with the bowed head.

KICKING BIRD
Your wounds are healing well? You are happy
to be here, with my family?

STANDS WITH A FIST
I am glad to be here. I am missing my husband.

Kicking Bird is leading up to something, and Stands With
A Fist fears it. She keeps her head bowed.

KICKING BIRD
We have word from many places that the whites are . . .

Kicking Bird stops himself. He knows this must be hard.
She brings her eyes to bear on the medicine man, waiting
to hear more.

KICKING BIRD

They are coming into everyone's country. They will soon be in ours, I think. This white man who lives at the old soldier fort, the one who calls himself Loo Ten Tant. . . . I have visited him and I believe his heart is a good one. He knows things about the whites which we do not.

He pauses, letting this sink in.

STANDS WITH A FIST

I am afraid of the man at the fort.

KICKING BIRD

He is only one man.

STANDS WITH A FIST

I am afraid that he will tell some whites that I am here. I am afraid that they will try to take me away.

KICKING BIRD
Every warrior in camp would fight them if they tried.

She is not much reassured by this. In the way of a defeatist, she lowers her eyes once more.

KICKING BIRD
I cannot make the white man talk. Loo Ten Tant does not know Sioux.

Kicking Bird waits. Still she does not raise her head.

KICKING BIRD
You have a certain medicine which no other Sioux— man or woman—has.

STANDS WITH A FIST
It has been a long time since I made the talk.

KICKING BIRD
I do not ask this for myself . . . I ask this for all our people.

STANDS WITH A FIST
It's dead in me.

KICKING BIRD
I want you to try and remember the words.

STANDS WITH A FIST
I don't know how.

KICKING BIRD
You don't want to know.

This outburst shocked Stands With A Fist. She ran out of the lodge and down to the river, weeping, her mind and heart in turmoil. As the storm of emotion passed, she grew quiet—then all at once she was back in the past, remembering for the first time the details of that long-ago day when the Pawnee came. How she'd been up on the sod roof with her young friend Willie while the Indians argued with her father. Her mother's screams after her father fell with a hatchet in his back, Willie kicking her off the roof and ordering her to run, anywhere. How she'd hidden in a cramped burrow on the prairie until the other Indians heard her desperate cries.

She hadn't been able to remember any English words until "Don't!" slipped out the day when the white soldier found her. Now they were in her head again. She did not know if her tongue would ever be able to make them, but she would try. She would try for the sake of Kicking Bird, who had argued for her life with the other Sioux when they had found the helpless child on the prairie . . . and who had cared for her in her recent trouble.

DUNBAR'S JOURNAL
"Two Socks, like Cisco, has become a trusted friend. He still won't eat from my hand, but his keen eyes and ears never fail to alert me when something is wrong."

The wolf suddenly stiffens, then slinks away through the grass. Dunbar sees what frightened Two Socks.

The escort has paused as usual on the brow of the hill. Today only Kicking Bird and Wind In His Hair ride forward. Kicking Bird is holding something large and bulky across his lap. It's a fine buffalo robe.

He hands the gift down into Dunbar's arms, who is entranced with it. Kicking Bird signs the question: "Have you seen buffalo?"

Dunbar sensed a certain desperation in the question. He told them he had food if they needed it, but Kicking Bird only shook his head and trotted back to the escort waiting on the bluff.

Scouts have picked up the trail...
a gigantic swath of torn-up ground
extending to the horizon. The sheer
numbers it took to create this
impossible image was hard to imagine.

PART III

Buffalo Hunt

Fort Sedgewick

[Dunbar's quarters]
It's night and the moon is full. As we look down on the
fort, we can hear a new sound coming off the prairie. A light
rumbling.

Lieutenant Dunbar is asleep in the moonlight. The
rumbling is getting louder. It wakes him. He gropes about,
lights the lantern and listens to the strange, powerful sound.

Something's in the air. He holds the lantern toward the
ceiling. Particles of dirt and dust are being shaken from the
roof. It's the earth that's trembling.

Going outside dressed only in his pants and boots,
Dunbar walks along the bluff above the river, his lantern
held out in front of him. The sound is tremendous now.
Dunbar stops as a great wall of dust rises before him. At the
same time, he realizes that something is alive behind the
wall of dust, and recognizes the sound . . . the sound of
thousands of hoofbeats.

He sees one veer out. And now another. And another,
darting briefly from the great cloud of dust. The most
powerful force on the prairie now seems like the most
powerful force on earth as it thunders by. The buffalo.

Without stopping to think, Dunbar bridled Cisco, vaulted onto his
bare back, and lit out like the devil was after him toward the Sioux

village. Horse and rider were soon racing through its outskirts toward a great fire, where many of the band were gathered.

Men wearing buffalo headdresses were dancing in the firelight, along with others. Dunbar couldn't pull Cisco up until he was in their midst, scattering the dancers. Cisco reared, and he slid onto the ground, where some of the warriors instantly set upon him. Only the intervention of Kicking Bird kept him from serious injury.

Trying to catch his breath, Dunbar gasped out the word he had learned for "buffalo," making the horn gesture with his fingers to emphasize the point. Finally Kicking Bird seemed to understand.

[Sioux village, fire]

KICKING BIRD
Buffalo?

DUNBAR
Yes. Buffalo. *Tatonka.*

Kicking Bird raises up and yells it out to his people.

KICKING BIRD
The buffalo have come!

For a fleeting moment there is shocked silence. Then the Sioux explode with excitement. Still dazed, Lieutenant Dunbar is pulled to his feet. The people are surging in around him with yelps of joy.

By dawn the next day, Ten Bears' camp was on the move. Nearly the entire village set off toward the hunting grounds. First came the lead scouts, followed by Ten Bears and his advisors, Kicking Bird and Wind In His Hair among them. A large body of warriors came next, then the women, children, and elderly. Dunbar rode at the head of the last group.

"Riders were sent out to pick up the trail. In the time it took to gather my things at Sedgewick, the entire tribe was on its way. The efficiency of the people and the speed at which they moved was enough to impress any military commander.

"Spirits are high and overnight I have gone from a person of suspicion to one of genuine standing. I am greeted with open smiles and looks of appreciation. In short, I have become a celebrity.

"Scouts have picked up the trail exactly where I said it would be. It was not hard to find . . . a gigantic swath of torn-up ground extending to the horizon. The sheer numbers it took to create this impossible image was hard to imagine."

Dunbar enjoyed the attention, but his own gaze kept wandering to Stands With A Fist, who rode near him. It was easier to see now that she had once been white.

Three far-ranging scouts came in at a run, and a few moments later, Wind In His Hair galloped off with a dozen warriors. Dunbar didn't know what was happening, but the faces of the men were suddenly stern instead of light-hearted. A little later, Kicking Bird motioned for the lieutenant to ride with him up to the front of the column.

Soon Dunbar could make out a strange sight up ahead—a series of pink bumps on the ground with black specks all around them. Then they were riding through the killing ground, where two dozen buffalo had been shot, stripped of their hides, and left to rot and scavengers. A doomed newborn calf bleated next to the body of its dead mother. The faces of the Sioux as they rode past were full of sorrow and anger.

"Who would do such a thing? The field was proof enough that it was a people without value and without soul, with

no regard for Sioux rights. The wagon tracks leading away left little doubt, and my heart sank as I knew it could only be white hunters.

"Voices that had been joyous all morning long were now as silent as the dead buffalo left to rot in this valley—killed only for their tongues and the price of their hides."

They rode on, and when they came near where the scouts estimated the buffalo would be, a temporary camp was pitched. Dunbar, Kicking Bird, and the scouts continued on to the base of a draw that led up to a bluff. Leaving their ponies tethered at the bottom, they clambered up the slope, dropping to their bellies as they neared the summit.

The line of men reached the crest together and peered over into an immense valley. There they were, by the thousands, grazing quietly in the twilight. The buffalo.

[Prairie]

The buffalo scouts, Dunbar included, are galloping back
to the temporary camp. It looms ahead of them, the hide-
covered lodges glowing like candles in the last light of day.
A big fire is blazing in the center of camp.

Dunbar hangs back as the other riders go into the noisy
camp. A special event of some kind is taking place. As he
looks the scene over, Dunbar sees something remarkable.
Back in the shadows, behind the fire, is a wagon.

Dunbar and Cisco pace back and forth on the fringes of
the camp. The lieutenant searches for any sign of the white
people who came in the wagon. Finding none, he focuses on
the dancers moving in a circle around the fire.

One of the men waving his lance is Wind In His Hair.
Dunbar's eyes track up the lance, and there he finds the
white people. Hanging from Wind In His Hair's lance tip
is a fresh scalp, blond and wavy. Several of the other men
have scalps too. None of the hair is Indian.

Dunbar slowly retreats into the shadows. Cisco is
hobbled nearby, and with the temporary camp glowing
on the plains a half-mile away, Dunbar spreads his blanket
on the open plain.

Dunbar was awakened at dawn by a moccasined foot poking into his
ribs. He looked up and saw Wind In His Hair standing over him with a
rifle, and thought perhaps his time had run out. But the warrior raised
his gun as if sighting at imaginary game, then lifted it overhead and
barked out a cry of victory. It was also an invitation.

[Temporary camp]

The band's best hunters, two dozen of them, are making ready to chase the buffalo. It's the big time; no event is more important. The villagers have gathered around each of the hunters.

The largest audience is clustered around Lieutenant Dunbar and Wind In His Hair. The warrior's pony is ready. Great bolts of yellow lightning adorn his shoulders and rump. Right now Wind In His Hair is drawing the same design along Cisco's rump.

Dunbar reads this correctly as a great honor and stands by silently. Wind In His Hair is finished. He looks at Dunbar and nods at the paint as if asking for a response.

IMI

DUNBAR
I wish I knew what to say.

A Sioux voice, using English words, sails out of the circle of watchers.

STANDS WITH A FIST
Say . . . thank you.

Startled, the men turn to the sound. The other Sioux are stunned too.

STANDS WITH A FIST
(indicating the paint) His speed . . . his power . . . you have.

DUNBAR
Thank you.

He takes the warrior's hand in his own and shakes it crisply.

The scene shifts to the buffalo herd. It's the first time we've seen the buffalo up close. They're fantastic creatures, powerful, brutish, untameable animals from another age. A great bull turns away from the others and lifts his purple, horned head to sniff the breeze. He can detect no sign of trouble and eventually returns to his browsing.

The hunters are advancing across the prairie, spreading out in a formation that will encircle part of the herd.

There's a lump in Dunbar's throat. He knows nothing of what is expected of him, but he's doing it anyway. He glances to his right at Wind In His Hair and to his left at Kicking Bird. They're both concentrating on what lies ahead. They are close enough now to hear the low bellowing of the herd. . . .

A strike far up on the horned formation. Their ponies leap forward. The mad dash is on.

Dunbar's hat flies off at first spurt, and now the lieutenant and his horse are hurtling over the prairie. The little buckskin seems to know what is expected of him and has put every ounce of muscle to speed. They're burning up the ground.

The herd is in full flight and the sound of their stampede is overwhelming. The buffalo are very fast but Cisco is gaining with every stride. They form a great running wall in front of him, and now Dunbar can see their rumps and tails and flying hooves. He takes a solid grip on his rifle and shuts his eyes as if in prayer. The sound of thousands of hooves is deafening.

Dunbar and Cisco have caught the buffalo. A few more strides and they'll be in. Now they're running in the herd.

A shaggy head moves in and swipes at Cisco, but the little horse is too quick and smart. He dodges away, nearly dumping the lieutenant in the process.

Dunbar rights himself and fires. It's a wild shot, only grazing the buffalo's shoulder. The report of the gun instantly scatters the herd, and Dunbar pulls up, dust swirling all around him.

Sioux hunters stream past him, every man for himself, zeroing in on targets. Dunbar starts to dismount, but something he sees stops him.

A hundred yards away, a small hunter is after a handful of buffalo that have splintered off from the rest. It's Smiles A Lot, trying to make a kill of his own. As Dunbar watches, the boy's inexperienced horse shies away and bucks, pitching the kid to the ground.

A big bull breaks away from the splinter group. Maddened by the sting of several arrows, he lowers his head, and charges. Dunbar spits a spare bullet from his mouth and rams it into the chamber.

Smiles A Lot is picking himself up off the ground. The bull is in full charge. Dunbar squeezes the trigger . . . and again . . . and again. The third bullet plows home, exploding the buffalo's heart. The big buffalo's legs collapse but the momentum of his charge puts him into a skid. He comes to rest only a few yards away from Smiles A Lot.

The boy stands as the lieutenant rides up. Smiles A Lot is dazed but he's okay.

Dunbar hops off next to the dead buffalo. He's a huge one, a real grandfather, and the lieutenant loses himself for a few moments in contemplation of this tremendous kill.

When he looks back, Smiles A Lot has caught his pony and is racing away from the scene of his humiliation.

The sounds of approaching riders turns Dunbar's attention in a different direction. The entire village is streaming onto the plains for the butchering. The riders bearing down on him are being lead by Wind In His Hair.

Wind In His Hair insisted that Dunbar take part in an age-old ritual of the kill. He sliced open the buffalo's belly, pulled out the still-warm liver, and took a large bite before offering it to the lieutenant. Dunbar had to force himself to taste it, but was astonished to find it delicious. He took a large bite and then raised the liver over his head in triumph as the onlookers cheered.

That night there was great feasting around the fires, as the best cuts of buffalo were cooked and consumed, and warriors wandered from group to group, recounting their tales of the hunt. Dunbar made the rounds with Wind In His Hair, until he thought his stomach and his head would explode if he had to eat another bite or tell his story one more time.

But Wind In His Hair wasn't ready to quit. On their way to the next campfire, Dunbar noticed the warrior eyeing his army tunic, and impulsively stripped it off and offered it to him. In return, Wind In His Hair insisted that Dunbar accept the magnificent bone breastplate he was wearing. Both men were delighted with the trade.

At the next feasting fire, the trading went on.

[Temporary camp]

As Dunbar gnaws on a rib, he glances at the friendly faces around the fire. His eyes suddenly stop their roving. A big warrior is wearing the military hat he lost on the hunt. It's a little too big. The brim touches the top of the warrior's ears.

Now the big warrior notices that Dunbar is staring at him. Their eyes meet.

DUNBAR
That's my hat.

At the sound of these words, the cheerful talk around the fire begins to fade. Dunbar touches the top of his head and points to his hat.

DUNBAR
My hat.

BIG WARRIOR
I found it on the prairie. It's mine.

A tense silence falls between the two men. Wind In His Hair stirs.

WIND IN HIS HAIR
That hat belongs to Loo Ten Tant.

BIG WARRIOR
He left it on the prairie. He didn't want it.

WIND IN HIS HAIR
You can see that he wants it now.

The big warrior shakes his head. He won't budge.

WIND IN HIS HAIR
We all know that it is a soldier hat. We all know who wears it. If you want to keep it, that's all right. But give something for it.

Some of the men around the fire murmur their assent. The big warrior thinks for a moment, then abruptly gets to his feet. He fumbles at his waist and unfastens a knife in a beautiful buckskin scabbard. He tosses it to Dunbar.

The lieutenant examines the item for a moment. Now he looks again at the big warrior. A smile breaks slowly across the Sioux's face, and Dunbar nods. At last he smiles back. It's a trade.

Staggering back to Kicking Bird's lodge, where he was to spend the night, Dunbar was invited to join a group of young girls dancing for their own pleasure. Reluctant at first, he picked up the steps quickly and started to enjoy himself. The touch of their bodies as they mischievously pressed closer in the circle was intoxicating to a man starved for female companionship.

Kicking Bird broke up the party, however, and escorted Dunbar to his lodge. Despite his exhaustion, the lieutenant was kept from sleep by the sounds of Kicking Bird and his wife, Black Shawl, making love . . . and by his awareness that Stands With A Fist was sleeping not far from him in the same lodge. At last he slept.

The butchering of the dead buffalo—perhaps seventy in all—took place each day right after the hunt. At each body, families set up portable factories that worked with amazing speed and precision in transforming animals into usable products. They took everything: hides, meat, guts, hooves, tails, heads. In the space of a few hours it was all gone, leaving the prairie with the appearance of a gigantic, recently cleared banquet table.

Finally the band broke camp and headed back to their home on the river. They dropped Lieutenant Dunbar off at Fort Sedgewick with a full travois of meat and went on their way. He had to keep looking at the travois to remind himself that the whole thing had been real and not a fantastic dream.

"It seems that every day ends with a miracle here, and whatever God may be, I thank God for this day. To stay any longer would have been useless. We had all the meat we could possibly carry. We had hunted for three days, losing a half a dozen ponies and only three men injured.

"I had never known a people so eager to laugh, so devoted to family, so dedicated to each other, and the only word that came to mind was harmony.

"Many times I have felt alone, but until this afternoon I have never felt completely lonely."

[Fort Sedgewick, bluff]

Two Socks has taken his dinner and retreated to the shadows. He munches contentedly until a strange sound jolts him to attention.

At the fort is an odd sight. Dunbar is dancing around the fire, occasionally singing out an energetic whoop.

Two Socks is caught up in the scene and lets out a howl of his own. It could be the Stone Age.

It was hard for Dunbar to reaccustom himself to his solitary routine at the fort after being in the thick of Indian society for several days. He was glad to see Two Socks, though, and the wolf seemed to feel likewise. One day the lieutenant found a freshly killed prairie chicken lying in front of his quarters and looked up to see Two Socks watching him from his usual place on the bluff.

"Made a long patrol today. There is nothing to report. The truth is, I am bored. Though only two days it seems like a week. I am missing the company of my new friends. I can see all of their faces, but somehow it is not enough.

*Tomorrow, I will make an unannounced visit. After all,
they are my neighbors, what can it hurt?"*

The next day, Dunbar and Cisco rode off toward the village. The
lieutenant looked very different than on the day when he set out with
his flag and polished buttons. Now his boots were worn and his striped
trousers faded almost to nothing. The bone breastplate shone in the
sun, and his rifle lay in the crook of his arm, Indian style.

He looked around and discovered that Two Socks was following him
at a discreet distance. He ordered him off, and the wolf stopped, but
when Cisco walked on, so did the wolf. Dunbar dismounted and tried a
few more times to shoo him away, but finally gave up. Two Socks' next
move in the game was to throw his head back and let loose with
a long, mournful howl.

[Prairie]
Like an angry father who's had too much, Dunbar charges
Two Socks with a roar.

DUNBAR
You go home!

The wolf races away this time, and Dunbar immediately
runs for Cisco, hoping to reach his horse and ditch Two
Socks. But he's not running long before the wolf comes
bouncing alongside. Dunbar weaves at him, startling Two
Socks. He sidles away, but as he does, the lieutenant reached
out and gives the base of his tail a good hard squeeze.

It might as well be a firecracker. Two Socks gives a yelp
and shoots off with his tail tucked. Dunbar laughs out loud.
He watches until the wolf has gone a fair distance without
sign of slowing down.

Still chuckling to himself, he turns once again and starts for Cisco at a trot. But moments later, something grabs at one of his ankles. The lieutenant's legs tangle and he goes down face first into the grass.

Lying on his belly not knowing what hit him, Dunbar rolls onto his side for a closer look. There's Two Socks, sitting in the grass a few feet back. Dunbar sits up cross-legged and smiles at his old friend.

Two Socks catches something suddenly, perhaps from a shift in the wind, and starts to slink away. Dunbar peers over the grass up at the bluff. It's Stone Calf, Kicking Bird, and Wind In His Hair. The Indian entourage is riding slowly toward Lieutenant Dunbar.

STONE CALF
You were right about Loo Ten Tant—he is a special white man.

Kicking Bird watches Dunbar as he replies.

KICKING BIRD
Yes, he is special . . . He should have a real name.

As I heard my Sioux name being
called over and over, I knew for
the first time who I really was.

PART IV

Dances With Wolves

Ten Bears' Village

Lieutenant Dunbar's arrival in the Sioux camp was different from the previous times. A group of young warriors rode out to meet him, full of cheer for a special friend, and most of the faces in the village were friendly. A few men hung back. Not everyone thought it was a good idea that he was there.

Kicking Bird sensed that the time had come to try his experiment of talking to Loo Ten Tant through Stands With A Fist. He escorted Dunbar into his tent and invited him to share in the pipe-smoking ritual. The tobacco was harsh but flavorful, and the beautiful pipe seemed almost alive in Dunbar's hand.

Then, to his surprise, the lodge flap opened and Stands With A Fist entered, seating herself between him and Kicking Bird. She looked much better than when he had first seen her—calmer and happier—and was dressed as if for a special occasion. He was glad to see her but wondered why she was there, until Kicking Bird looked at him and spoke to him in Lakota.

[Kicking Bird's lodge]

KICKING BIRD
Welcome. It is good that you are here.

Kicking Bird looks to Stands With A Fist. She takes her time, and the words are accented, but they are close enough.

STANDS WITH A FIST
Hullo. You are here . . . good.

The words are sweet music to the lieutenant. He replies with a feeling of great relief.

DUNBAR
Thank you . . . I feel good.

STANDS WITH A FIST
(to Kicking Bird) He thanks you. It is good.

KICKING BIRD
Ask him why he is at the soldier fort.

STANDS WITH A FIST
(to Dunbar) Uhh . . . you . . . come . . .

But Dunbar jumped in before she could finish. There were things he had wanted to know for a long time. He asked what her name was, and Kicking Bird agreed that introductions should come first. The girl haltingly pieced the Sioux names together for him, and when he inquired if Kicking Bird was a chief, she explained that he was a "holy man." Then he introduced himself.

DUNBAR
Stands With A Fist. I am John Dunbar.

Rediscovering her English tongue was a source of great excitement to Stands With A Fist, and she was reluctant to end the first session. For Kicking Bird it was a breakthrough—not only in his friendship with the white soldier, but for his hopes to learn information vital to his people. For Dunbar, it opened a world that until now he could only observe from the outside.

Dunbar slept that night in Kicking Bird's lodge, and for many nights thereafter. The better he came to know Kicking Bird, the more he

respected the medicine man's intelligence. But he found himself having to sidestep the issue that Kicking Bird always returned to.

DUNBAR'S JOURNAL

"I try to answer all of Kicking Bird's questions, but I know he is frustrated with me. He always wants to know how many more white people are coming. I tell him it is impossible for me to say. When he persists, I tell him that the white people will most likely pass through this country and nothing more.

"But I am speaking to him in half-truths. One day there will be too many, but I cannot bring myself to tell him that. I am sure that Stands With A Fist knows."

Before long, Dunbar had his own lodge near the outer perimeter of the camp. He continued to go back to the fort—to keep an eye on things, make repairs where needed, note events in his journal. Deeply involved as he was with the Sioux, he could not bring himself to entirely abandon his identity as Lieutenant John J. Dunbar, U.S.A. He was two people now, like Stands With A Fist. From the waist up, with his untrimmed hair and bone breastplate, he was beginning to resemble an Indian. But he still wore his striped Army pants and tall black boots.

> **DUNBAR'S JOURNAL**
> *"A war party is going against the Pawnee soon, and I have asked to go. I sensed that I have made a mistake in doing so, but I could not bring myself to take it back. They are my friends, and from what little I gather, the Pawnee have been very hard on these people. I hope I have not overstepped my bounds."*

[Dunbar's lodge]

It is night, inside Dunbar's lodge. His surroundings are completely Indian. He is cleaning the big Navy revolver. The lodge flap rustles, and in come Stands With A Fist and Kicking Bird. Dunbar stands to greet them.

> **DUNBAR**
> I am glad to see you . . . please sit.

Kicking Bird speaks and Stands With A Fist translates.

> **STANDS WITH A FIST**
> Kicking Bird wants to know why you want to make war on the Pawnee. They have done nothing to you.

> **DUNBAR**
> They are Sioux enemies.

STANDS WITH A FIST

(translating) Only Sioux warriors will go.

DUNBAR

I asked that he would think about my going.

STANDS WITH A FIST

He has.

DUNBAR

Then tell him this. I have been a warrior longer than many of the young men that will go on this war party. Tell him.

STANDS WITH A FIST

He says that the Sioux way of being a warrior is not the white way. You are not ready.

DUNBAR

I know, I understand. But I cannot learn these ways in camp.

She translates this to Kicking Bird. The medicine man hesitates, then speaks once more.

STANDS WITH A FIST

He asks that you watch over his family while he is gone.

Dunbar looks to Kicking Bird, then to Stands With A Fist, unable to mask his disappointment.

STANDS WITH A FIST

(on her own) This thing he asks you . . . it is a great honor for you.

Dunbar thinks a moment longer and speaks directly to Kicking Bird.

> **DUNBAR**
> I will be happy to watch over your family.

> **STANDS WITH A FIST**
> *(translating)* He thanks Dances With Wolves for coming.

> **DUNBAR**
> Who is Dances With Wolves?

> **STANDS WITH A FIST**
> It is the name which all the people are calling you now.

He thinks and remembers the episode with Two Socks.

> **DUNBAR**
> Dances With Wolves . . . that's right . . . that day.
> *(to Stands With A Fist)* How do you say it?

> **STANDS WITH A FIST**
> *(in Lakota)* Dances With Wolves.

> **DUNBAR**
> *(in Lakota to Kicking Bird)* Dances With Wolves.

The medicine man smiles.

The war party of twenty warriors—the band's best fighters—left to seek out the Pawnee. Kicking Bird and Wind In His Hair were among them. There were no tears among the families left behind, although they knew some might not return.

Dances With Wolves still wished he could go with them, but his regret was tempered by the pleasure he had come to take in the company of Stands With A Fist and their lessons. He made rapid progress in learning the Lakota language. She too had begun to look forward eagerly to their time together and to feel anxious whenever he made his periodic trips back to Fort Sedgewick. Black Shawl knew the girl well and noticed the change in her.

One morning Dances With Wolves was waiting for her on Cisco outside Kicking Bear's lodge when she emerged, carrying a couple of water bags.

[Kicking Bird's lodge]

DANCES WITH WOLVES
You go for water?

His Lakota is perfect, and she smiles.

STANDS WITH A FIST
Yes.

DANCES WITH WOLVES
Let us take you.

Cisco makes his way down the river trail. He shies at the flurry of wings as a covey of quail flies up before them. Stands With A Fist tightens her grip around Dances With Wolves' waist.

When they reach the riverbank, she draws water into a set of bladder bags. Dances With Wolves squats next to her, staring at the eddying stream.

DANCES WITH WOLVES
How did you get your name?

STANDS WITH A FIST

I was not very old when I came to be with the people . . . I was made to work.

She lugs the filled bags onto shore and sits next to Dances With Wolves.

STANDS WITH A FIST

I worked every day . . . very hard . . . there was a woman who didn't like me. She called me bad names . . . sometimes she beat me. One day she was calling me these bad names, her face in my face, and I hit her. I was not very big, but she fell down. She fell hard and didn't move. I stood over her with my fist and asked if any other woman wanted to call me bad names . . .

   (laughing at the recollection) No one bothered me after that day.

DANCES WITH WOLVES

I would not think so.

A little silence.

DANCES WITH WOLVES

Show me where you hit her.

He taps his jaw. She makes a fist and brushes very gently at the point of his jaw. Dances With Wolves' eyes flutter. They roll up in his head and he keels over backward . . . out cold. She goes with the joke. Bending over him, she slaps lightly at each side of his cheeks, until Dances With Wolves revives. He sits up, rubbing his jaw.

   Neither acknowledges the joke, and a sudden awkward-

ness falls between them. Stands With A Fist fiddles shyly
with the ties on the water bags, while Dances With Wolves
draws lines in the earth with a stick. Finally he works up the
courage to ask a delicate question.

> DANCES WITH WOLVES
> Why are you not married?

The question comes as a jolt to Stands With A Fist. She
stops her fiddling. A visible stiffness overtakes her. She
quickly stands up.

> STANDS WITH A FIST
> I must go.

Dances With Wolves doesn't know what to do. He only
knows that he should not have asked the question. She
slings the heavy bags over her shoulders and starts back
up the path. Dances With Wolves jumps to his feet.

> DANCES WITH WOLVES
> I'm sorry. Let me help . . .

But the words are delivered to her back. She is already
hurrying up the path with her heavy load.

For the next few days, Dances With Wolves did not find Stands With A
Fist where they were accustomed to meet. He was troubled, and sought
out Stone Calf, one of the elders left behind in the village and a close
friend of Ten Bears.

[Stone Calf's lodge]
Dances With Wolves sits in the shade with Stone Calf,

watching the older man painting a design on a new shield.

> STONE CALF
> Some of your words are wrong . . . but you are
> learning fast. That is good. What can I tell you today?

Dances With Wolves is a little taken aback. The elder has read his mind. He decides to speak it.

> DANCES WITH WOLVES
> I want to know about Stands With A Fist.

For the first time, Stone Calf leaves his work. He gives his visitor a quick and penetrating look. Then he goes back to his shield.

> STONE CALF
> What is your question?

> DANCES WITH WOLVES
> There is no man with her.

Stone Calf considers before he speaks. It is not something he wants to get into.

> STONE CALF
> She is in mourning.

> DANCES WITH WOLVES
> I do not understand "mourning."

> STONE CALF
> She is crying for someone.

> DANCES WITH WOLVES
> Crying for who?

STONE CALF
It is not polite to speak of the dead . . . but I will tell
you . . . you are new. She cries for her husband. He
was killed not long ago.

The blood has gone out of Dances With Wolves' face. He
tries to digest this.

DANCES WITH WOLVES
How long will she cry?

STONE CALF
It is Kicking Bird's place to say when she is finished.

It would take Dances With Wolves a little time and distance to figure
out how to react to this news. He set out for the fort again, a trip he felt
he would be making for the last time.

Stands With A Fist went for comfort to Black Shawl. Sorting out
her confused feelings, she realized that she had hurt Dances With
Wolves, and now she wanted to talk to him. But Black Shawl told her
he had already left the village, and after racing to his lodge to see for
herself, she finally broke down and cried in the older woman's arms.

At Fort Sedgewick, Dances With Wolves made a cursory inspection.
The fort was beginning to show signs of neglect. Inside his old quarters,
he leafed through his beloved journal, smiling at some of the memories.
Finding pen and ink, he wrote on a blank page near the end,
"I love Stands With A Fist," and signed himself "Dances With
Wolves." Something stirred outside, and he moved cautiously
out to check.

[Fort Sedgewick]
Lying in the sun a few feet away is Two Socks. He looks up

hopefully at Dances With Wolves. The two partners stare at
each other for a moment.

Then Dances With Wolves reaches into a little day
pouch at his side and pulls out a strip of jerky. He squats
close to the ground and offers the meat to the wolf.

Two Socks is up now. He takes several tentative steps.
His nose sniffs at the meat and he opens his mouth. Teeth
and fingers touch as the wolf takes the meat delicately. Now,
in his customary style, he moves away, heading out onto the
prairie with his prize.

Dances With Wolves watches a moment longer. Then he vaults onto Cisco's back and they canter off in the direction of the village.

[Riverside near camp]
Stands With A Fist is wading through the water, her mind far away.

In a moment there is a shift in the wind. The rustling of the trees alerts her to a presence she had not thought to feel before. Gradually she raises her eyes to see the figure of a man moving through the trees . . . Dances With Wolves.

Stands With A Fist walks slowly out of the water. He opens his arms and she melts into them, letting her head rest against his chest.

STANDS WITH A FIST
I am in mourning.

DANCES WITH WOLVES
I know . . . Stone Calf told me.

She presses her body against him, feeling all of him.

STANDS WITH A FIST
No one can know . . . we must be careful.

DANCES WITH WOLVES
Yes.

She climbs higher into his arms for a moment. Then, supporting each other, the lovers move into the cover of the willow breaks along the river.

They continued to meet in the days to come, in public for lessons, secretly for love. It is doubtful whether Black Shawl was fooled, but she said nothing. It would be her husband's responsibility to settle the matter when he returned.

One night their lovemaking was interrupted by a disturbance outside. Several strange warriors rode into camp, with one pony carrying a dead man. They were Kiowa, sometime allies of the Sioux.

[Sioux village]
Dances With Wolves hurries through a light rain to the scene of a commotion going on in Ten Bears' lodge. There's a real sense of panic in the air by the time he reaches the fire outside the lodge.

It's a wild scene. Ten Bears is trying to huddle with his advisors, the wounded men are trying to tend their injuries, and the rest of the warriors in camp are holding little skull sessions amid much shouting. Women are running to and fro, rounding up their children.

Dances With Wolves spots Stands With A Fist making her way toward him. Her eyes are big with terror.

STANDS WITH A FIST
Pawnee . . . a big party . . . thirty or forty men . . . *(indicating wounded)*
   The Kiowa hunters found them not far to the north. The Pawnee are coming this way. Soon they will find our camp.

Stone Calf is just passing by. Dances With Wolves stops him.

DANCES WITH WOLVES
Stone Calf . . . I follow you.

The older man doesn't mince words.

STONE CALF
The Pawnee do not come for horses, they come for blood . . . and with many men gone, we are few.

Dances With Wolves nods.

STONE CALF
Get your weapons and come to my lodge.

Suddenly an inspiration hit Dances With Wolves. Weapons . . . he had weapons! Good Army rifles, dozens of them, carefully cached in the ground around Fort Sedgewick. Quickly he explained the situation to Ten Bears and Stone Calf, and though the chief was at first reluctant to spare any men for the journey, he finally agreed to let Dances With Wolves take one other.

The teenaged Smiles A Lot had overheard, and stepped forward silently. An hour later, the two were combing the landscape around the fort. The weather had worsened, and they could barely see through the driving rain and intermittent flashes of lightning. At last Smiles A Lot heard something snap under his pony's hoof, and discovered the buffalo rib Dunbar had used to mark his weapons cache.

Dragging the wooden crates on a travois, they neared the villlage at dawn. In the illumination from a flash of lightning, they saw the Pawnee crossing the river only a mile or so upstream of the camp.

At a quick battle meeting, the guns and ammunition were distributed, and Dances With Wolves demonstrated their use.

Dances With Wolves steps into Kicking Bird's lodge, followed by Smiles A Lot. They both have rifles, and Dances With Wolves' old long-barreled revolver is holstered at his waist.

Before him is a quiet, tense scene. The women are huddled together on a single sleeping platform. Kicking Bird's three children are nestled between them. Two of the kids are crying softly.

Black Shawl grips a hatchet and Stands With A Fist has a rifle. They will both fight. But they are both scared. Everyone in the village has a life at stake. In one glimpse, Dances With Wolves understands what he will be fighting for. He looks once more at the women and children, and ducks out of the lodge.

It has stopped raining, but the ground is still soaked and an early morning fog is swirling through the camp. Clumped in groups of five or six, behind the lodges nearest the river, are Sioux warriors with rifles. They're absolutely quiet as they wait for the enemy.

Dances With Wolves looks across a clearing that slopes down to the breaks fronting the river. Nothing.

The Pawnee are visible now, a war party at its fiercest, painted and feathered and armed to the teeth. Coming on foot, the first of them have reached the edge of the clearing. They start into a stealthy trot, more and more of them breaking into a run.

A Pawnee war cry goes up, and as the others join in, Ten Bears lowers his hand. In ragged formation, the Sioux pour from behind the lodges, and thirty rifles fire into the vanguard of the Pawnee charge.

The smoke of many rifles mingles with the ground fog as the Sioux run screaming down on the Pawnee. Dances With Wolves screams too as he runs flat out down the slope.

While hand-to-hand fighting raged furiously in the clearing, some of the Pawnee made their way to the lodges where the women and children hid. A Pawnee warrior tried to enter Kicking Bird's lodge, but Stands With a Fist's rifle drove him back. . . .

A wounded and angry Pawnee staggered into Ten Bears' lodge, his hatchet raised to cut down those within. An arrow from Stone Calf's bow, fired from the entrance, stopped him, and Ten Bears' wife, Pretty Shield, finished him off with a half-burned log from the fire. . . .

Dances With Wolves fought in the clearing, and killed one Pawnee with his revolver. Suddenly he was bumped from behind and knocked to his knees.

[Battlefield]
It's a frantic Pawnee war horse, loose on the battlefield. Dances With Wolves grabs a hunk of mane and swings onto his back.

He has a real view now. The Pawnee are taking a terrible licking. Already they are being beaten back to the river. A turbaned enemy is falling back toward the river, firing arrows as he goes. Dances With Wolves goes after him. . . .

Stone Calf, his bow and arrow at the ready, is looking for more enemies to kill. Suddenly from the corner of his eye, the old man senses an attack. But he is too late. A Pawnee war club crushes his skull and the old man collapses.

Now we can see his attacker. It is the fierce Pawnee warrior who killed Timmons, the wagon driver. He glowers

down at the body of Stone Calf and swings his club at the old man's head once more.

Dances With Wolves squints toward the village just in time to see The Toughest take another shot at the prostrate, white-headed form of Stone Calf. He begins to run.

The Toughest has his knife to Stone Calf's forehead, and is preparing to scalp his victim when something strikes him in the lower leg. He looks down to find a small arrow embedded in his calf. He looks up to see three boys,

Otter, Worm, and Smiles A Lot, huddled at the edge of the battlefield.

Their faces go ashen as The Toughest bears down on them. Otter's arrow flies weakly into the air. The boys turn and run for their lives.

The Toughest would catch them with ease, but now he sees half a dozen howling Sioux warriors angling in to cut him off. He knows in a glance that the fight has been lost. He also knows that he can still escape if he changes direction. He veers for the river.

Sioux warriors on horse and foot race along the river-bank to block his retreat. Soon he is surrounded, and the circle slowly tightens as he wheels his pony in the center, seeking an opening.

Finally he accepts his fate. Lofting his war club in the air, he looses a last defiant scream as many rifles speak at once. Then they are on him, taking their revenge.

All at once the battle was over. The Pawnee attackers lay where they had fallen, while the Sioux victors leaped around in high spirits, finishing off the wounded and counting coup on the dead. Dances With Wolves caught a glimpse of Stone Calf's body in Ten Bears' arms. Then the Sioux warriors gathered around him, chanting his name and acknowledging his part in the victory.

DUNBAR (INTERNAL)
"It was hard to know how to feel. I had never been in a battle like this one. This had not been a fight for territory or riches or to make men free. This battle had no ego. It had been fought to preserve the food stores that would see us through the winter, to protect the lives of women and

children and loved ones only a few feet away. I felt a pride
I had never felt before.

"I had never really known who John Dunbar was.
Perhaps because the name itself had no meaning. But
as I heard my Sioux name being called over and over,
I knew for the first time who I really was."

The war party led by Kicking Bird and Wind In His Hair was met
outside the village by riders bringing news of the successful defense.
The medicine man gave a celebration dinner that night for Dances
With Wolves and other prominent warriors, but Dances With Wolves
excused himself early to be with Stands With A Fist.

Black Shawl was the only one to notice that the girl slipped out of
Kicking Bird's lodge shortly after Dances With Wolves, and raised the
subject later that night.

[Kicking Bird's lodge]
The medicine man's wife is already in bed as he slips under
the covers with a grunt.

BLACK SHAWL
How long will Stands With A Fist mourn?

Kicking Bird gives his wife an odd look.

KICKING BIRD
I don't know.

BLACK SHAWL
I hope it will not be too long.

Kicking Bird rises on his elbows.

KICKING BIRD
Something has happened? Well, what?

BLACK SHAWL
She has found love again.

KICKING BIRD
With who?

BLACK SHAWL
Danccs With Wolves.

KICKING BIRD
Are you certain of this?

BLACK SHAWL
When you see them together you will know.

Kicking Bird stares wearily across the floor.

KICKING BIRD
What are people saying? They're not angry?

BLACK SHAWL
No. They like the match. It makes sense. They are
both white.

KICKING BIRD
I suppose I will be the one to say something.

BLACK SHAWL
Relax, you can't see everything coming.

The next day, Kicking Bird intercepted Stands With A Fist on her way
back to the lodge with an armload of firewood.

KICKING BIRD
Stands With A Fist.

STANDS WITH A FIST
Yes.

KICKING BIRD
You will mourn no more.

He turns abruptly and stalks off, leaving the girl to ponder the meaning of his curt announcement. A smile gradually works onto her face.

So the match is made and a wedding day set. Just before the ceremony, Wind In His Hair came to find his friend.

[Dances With Wolves' lodge]
Dances with Wolves' hair is shiny. His breastplate gleams. The officer's pants have been dusted, and his old boots have something resembling a shine. The groom is ready.

WIND IN HIS HAIR
Pretty good . . .

A brief silence as Wind In His Hair contemplates something he wants to say.

WIND IN HIS HAIR
You know, the man she mourned for was my best friend.

DANCES WITH WOLVES
I didn't know that.

WIND IN HIS HAIR
He was a good man. It has been hard for me to like you. I am not the thinker Kicking Bird is. I always feel anger first. There were no answers to my

questions. But now I think he went away because you were coming. That is how I see it.

The sound of music and people outside distracts both men. Kicking Bird is leading the wedding party. Stands With A Fist is by his side. She glows with the special beauty of a bride.

Kicking Bird steps forward, his wife and Stands With A Fist following in his footsteps.

KICKING BIRD
This is a good day for me.

DANCES WITH WOLVES
And for me.

KICKING BIRD
Stands With A Fist . . . if you want this man, take his hand in yours.

Shyly she holds out a slender, graceful hand. Dances With Wolves meets it with one of his own.

The medicine man looks his friend in the eyes for several seconds.

Dances With Wolves also begins to speak . . . internally. At first the volume of his voice and that of the medicine man are nearly equal, but Kicking Bird's voice quickly begins to fade.

DUNBAR (INTERNAL)
"I had never been married before. I don't know if all grooms have the same experience. But as Kicking Bird began to speak about what was expected of a Sioux husband, my mind began to swim in a way that shut out everything but her. The tiny details of her costume. The contours of her

shape. The light in her eyes. The smallness of her feet.
I knew that the love between us would be served."

The chill of the coming winter was in the air, and Dances With Wolves and Stands With A Fist spent a lot of time in their lodge. The word around the village was that they were trying to make a baby.

One day shortly before the band was due to move to their winter camp, Kicking Bird came to visit Dances With Wolves.

> KICKING BIRD
> I am riding today to a far away place. It is a place I haven't seen for a long time. A sacred place. I would like you to come with me.

Later they are cantering side by side across the open prairie. They pull their horses to a walk, and Kicking Bird glances in Dances With Wolves' direction. Dances With Wolves looks back and smiles.

> DANCES WITH WOLVES
> It's good to be out.

> KICKING BIRD
> Yes, it must be.

> DANCES WITH WOLVES
> We are trying for a baby.

> KICKING BIRD
> No waiting?

> DANCES WITH WOLVES
> No waiting.

The medicine man keeps looking at his protege. There is virtually no semblance of Lieutenant Dunbar left.

KICKING BIRD

I was just thinking that of all the trails in this life, there is one that matters more than all the others. It is the trail of a true human being. I think you are on this trail, and it is good to see.

Dances With Wolves memorized these words and kept them in his heart. But he told no one, not even Stands With A Fist. He made them part of his private medicine.

*I must try and talk
to those who would listen...*

PART V

Like the Stars

On the prairie

Dances With Wolves and Kicking Bird rode for half a day southeast from the village to reach the place Kicking Bird had spoken of. Finally, at the crest of a steep hill, they saw the curving line of a river below them. It was screened by a mammoth stand of trees, some of them towering a hundred feet or more.

> [Prairie]
> Dances With Wolves is staring in wonder at the great forest before him.

>> **KICKING BIRD**
>> It is said that all the animals were born here . . . that from here they spread over the prairies to feed the people. Even our enemies say this is a sacred place.

> They start toward the river, and soon the two riders come out of the sunlight and onto a shaded path leading into the forest. They've gone only a few yards when Kicking Bird pulls to a stop. The men sit on their horses in complete silence. Dances With Wolves is still fully entranced.

>> **DANCES WITH WOLVES**
>> It's quiet.

> But Kicking Bird does not acknowledge his companion's words. He seems to be concentrating on the quiet. The

quiet is wrong and Kicking Bird knows it. He moves forward slowly.

When they reached the heart of the forest, a beautiful, cathedral-like clearing, they found that it had been horribly desecrated. Trees had been felled everywhere for no explicable reason, most of them left to rot. The quiet was replaced by the loud buzzing of flies hovering over the carcasses of dozens of small mammals—badgers, skunks, and squirrels—nearly all of them killed for target practice. The bodies of many deer were strewn around, choice portions cut off here and there but most senselessly mutilated.

Riding through the carnage in a sad daze, the men discovered a few crudely thrown-together shelters, whiskey bottles scattered on the ground outside, and a great pile of wild turkeys off to one side, not even plucked.

The anger rose in Dances With Wolves, and he wanted to wait for whoever had done this. But Kicking Bird noted that the place had not been inhabited for a week or more. So they watered their horses and turned back toward home.

They paused for a rest late in the day. Both men were sick at heart from what they had witnessed, and Dances With Wolves felt great shame for his own race. When he finally spoke, it was to answer a question that had hung between him and his friend for a long time.

[Prairie]

DANCES WITH WOLVES
You have asked me many times about the white people...you always ask how many more are coming.

He looks at his friend and mentor.

DANCES WITH WOLVES
There will be a lot, my friend . . . more than can
be counted.

KICKING BIRD
Help me to know how many.

DANCES WITH WOLVES
Like the stars.

This is what Kicking Bird wanted to know. And it hits him
like a rock. He bows his head in thought while Dances With
Wolves raises his. He never wanted to say this, he wishes it
wasn't true.

DANCES WITH WOLVES
It makes me afraid for all the Sioux.

When they got back to camp, they went to Ten Bears to report on
the desecration of the forest and talk about Dances With Wolves'
prediction.

The old man just puffed away on his pipe in silence for some time.
Then he got up and reached into the sacred rigging above his bedside,
taking down a melon-sized bundle, which he brought back to the
fire and slowly unwrapped. Dances With Wolves recognized the
rusted hulk of metal inside from pictures he had seen. It was a
conquistador's helmet.

[Ten Bears' lodge]

TEN BEARS
The men who wore this came in the time of my
grandfather's grandfather. Eventually we drove them

out. Then the Mexicans came. They do not come here anymore. In my own time, the Texans. They have been like all the others.

But I think you are right. I think they will keep coming. When I think of that, I look at this helmet. I don't know if we are ready for these people. But our country is all that we have, and we will fight to keep it.

Tomorrow we will strike the village and go to the winter camp.

Dances With Wolves was relieved to be going. Soon, he hoped, they would have a child, and it troubled him to think of white hunters just half a day's ride from the village. There was no question in his mind about staying with the band . . . there was nothing of himself left back at Fort Sedgewick.

He and Stands With A Fist joined in the fevered preparations for departure. But just as the band was ready to move out, he remembered —his journal was still somewhere at the fort. He found Kicking Bird and quickly explained to him.

DANCES WITH WOLVES
The words in the book are like a trail for people to follow. It tells everything about my life here. I must get it.

KICKING BIRD
We cannot wait for you.

Dances With Wolves vowed to catch up as soon as his errand was done. Swinging onto Cisco, he rode hard for Fort Sedgewick, and topped the last rise at a full run.

The sight of soldiers at the fort shocked him so much that he couldn't react right away. There must have been forty or fifty bluecoats going about their tasks, including a group in a wagon very close by. In a heartbeat, they had seen him and scrambled for their guns, screaming out the alarm: "Indians!"

As he fought to pull Cisco up, the buckskin reared high in the air, then fell heavily as a volley was fired from the wagon. Dances With Wolves hit the ground hard, and when he collected his senses, all he could see was his beloved horse lying still. He crawled over to make sure he was dead, then whirled to face the soldiers racing to surround him. A rifle stock slammed into his face, and everything went black.

[Sioux caravan]

Ten Bears' village is on the trail. Kicking Bird is riding down the line. He notices Stands With A Fist. She is terribly distraught.

Kicking Bird glances at the sun. The day is more than half over. He kicks his pony back up the line next to Wind In His Hair.

KICKING BIRD
Something has happened . . . Dances With Wolves is not coming.

WIND IN HIS HAIR
He must have trouble.

KICKING BIRD
Pick two men with fast ponies and send them back to the soldier fort.

Dances With Wolves awoke on the floor of his old supply hut, his face swollen and bloody. The soldiers guarding him alerted their officers, who soon arrived to question him. They seemed to doubt whether he could speak English, and reacted in astonishment when he identified himself.

DANCES WITH WOLVES
I am Lieutenant John J. Dunbar. This is my post.

MAJOR
Why are you dressed like this?

DANCES WITH WOLVES
I came out from Fort Hays last April. But there was no one here.

He directed them to look at his journal for proof of what he said. The young Lieutenant Elgin ordered a search for it, but it could not be found. A sly private named Spivey had already found it and hidden it for his own uses, though he didn't know what those might be.

Dances With Wolves was not treated gently by his captors, nor was he a docile prisoner. The next time they came to interrogate him, he tried to get information out of them.

ELGIN
Why are you out of uniform?

DANCES WITH WOLVES
What is the army doing out here?

Sergeant Bauer shoves Dances With Wolves with his gun.

BAUER
Lieutenant's askin' the questions here.

Elgin quickly steps in.

ELGIN
We are charged with apprehending hostiles,
recovering stolen property, and retrieving white
captives taken in hostile raidings.

DANCES WITH WOLVES
There are no hostiles.

MAJOR
We will ascertain that for ourselves. Now if you
guide us to these camps and serve as an interpreter,
your conduct will be reevaluated.

DANCES WITH WOLVES
What conduct?

MAJOR

Your status as a traitor might improve, should you
choose to cooperate with the United States Army.

DANCES WITH WOLVES

(quietly) There is nothing for you to do out here.

Elgin can see that the major's attitude and inexperience have
killed any chance of communication. He makes one last try
on his own.

ELGIN

Are you willing to cooperate or not?

MAJOR

Well, speak up . . .

DANCES WITH WOLVES

(softly in Lakota) I am Dances With Wolves . . .

MAJOR

What's that?

DANCES WITH WOLVES

(loudly in Lakota) I am Dances With Wolves . . .
I have nothing to say to you. You are not worth
talking to.

The major in command didn't like the idea of keeping this difficult
prisoner around. Clearly the renegade would die before helping them.
He resolved to ship him back to Fort Hays immediately, thereby
both ridding himself of a nuisance and getting credit for capturing
a "hostile."

Sioux scouts had observed Dances With Wolves being escorted roughly down to the river to wash the blood from his battered face. They raced back to the band, still on the march to winter camp, and reported the situation. Wind In His Hair quickly assembled a party of six warriors to ride to the fort. They would stay in hiding until some opportunity presented itself to get Dances With Wolves away from the white soldiers. Smiles A Lot begged to go with them, and Wind In His Hair assented—but the boy was only coming to hold the horses, he warned.

[Fort Sedgewick]
The wagon is pulling out with an escort of seven soldiers.

Dances With Wolves' spirits are very low as he sits in the bed of the jolting wagon, his hands manacled. Spivey is guarding him. Elgin is leading the detail.

Dances With Wolves watches a ridge in the distance for any sign of riders.

But the first being they encountered, not far from the fort, was Two Socks, who had spotted the wagon and come closer to investigate. Even when the soldiers went for their rifles and fired at him, the wolf didn't flee. His instinct to fear men had been blunted.

Dances With Wolves spoiled Spivey's shot by yanking his feet out from under him, and paid for it with a blow from Sergeant Bauer's rifle stock. But it wasn't long before one of the soldiers found the range. Two of them leaped from the wagon to retrieve their quarry, but Elgin ordered them back. The wagon rumbled on past Two Socks' body.

[Riverbank]

The wagon is making its way steadily down toward the river. Dances With Wolves watches the line of growth along the riverbank get closer, his eyes and ears and nose fully alert.

If they come, this will be the place to do it. Dances With Wolves will make the most of this hope.

The lieutenant raises his hand, and the wagon halts at the river's edge. A soldier rides back and forth in the water near the other side, checking for any signs of ambush. The soldier starts back, signaling "all clear."

The wagon was in the middle of the river when the Sioux struck. Lieutenant Elgin received the first arrow, and the outrider was next to go. Wind In His Hair came on, leading six warriors.

Dances With Wolves looped his shackles around Spivey's neck in a death grip. Seeing Sergeant Bauer take aim at the approaching riders, he kicked out viciously, sending Bauer over the side of the wagon. Then he snapped his tormentor's neck as the other Sioux made short work of the remaining soldiers.

[River]

In the midst of the smoke and confusion of the battle, Bauer has made his way to the cover of the weeds along the riverbank. Crashing through the thicket, he comes

to a clearing, and there in the shallows comes face to face
with Smiles A Lot.

The boy is standing there holding the extra horses, so
frightened by the sight of this white soldier that he doesn't
move. Bauer sticks his revolver into Smiles A Lot's face and
pulls the trigger. But the hammer only clicks. Bauer pistol-
whips the boy, knocking him to the ground, and grabs for
the closest of the horses. But the ponies are all stirred up
now and start to run down the river.

Bauer hears a bone-chilling whoop. Wind In His Hair is
coming. His pony plows through the water at full speed. A
skull-cracker dangles from one hand. The warrior begins to
whirl it around.

Terrified, Bauer turns to run. Before he can take a step, a hatchet buries itself to the hilt. Smiles A Lot is at the other end.

Wind In His Hair rides up and voices an approving whoop for the boy's first kill.

With Bauer's death, it was all over. Searching Elgin's body, Dances With Wolves and Wind In His Hair found the key to the shackles. The warrior stripping Spivey's body didn't notice something fall from the pocket of his tunic. John Dunbar's journal floated gently away on the river's current.

[Prairie]
The rescue party is cantering across the prairie.

DANCES WITH WOLVES
(to Wind In His Hair) We go south?

WIND IN HIS HAIR
We will ride south for two days . . . then turn east.
No one must follow.

This doesn't seem to bother Wind In His Hair. But it sets Dances With Wolves to thinking.

[Winter camp]
The sound of a single drum calls attention to eight silhouettes on horseback making their way down the ridge. The entire village begins to rumble with excitement as the news spreads.

The rescue party is walking down the trail single file. Dances With Wolves is a few slots back. The village is racing up the canyon to greet them. Stands With A Fist leads them all.

The band settled in for the long winter. Their camp was on the floor of a steep-walled canyon in the mountains, sheltered from the prairie winds and well-hidden. There was plenty of wood for fires, and the hunting had supplied them with enough meat to last through the season.

The general feeling of well-being and security was not shared by Dances With Wolves. The fear in his heart could not be dismissed, and he could see no way out of making the hardest choice of his life. He finally talked it over with Stands With A Fist, and she understood. It was simple for her: Whatever he decided to do, she would be with him.

After that, he went to talk with his friends.

[Ten Bears' lodge]
Several men are gathered around Ten Bears' fire, including Kicking Bird, Wind In His Hair, and Dances With Wolves. All the men are draped in blankets. The wind is howling outside. The men are engaged in small talk as the pipe goes around the circle.

The pipe comes around to Dances With Wolves, and the man next to him must nudge him to attention. Dances With Wolves takes the pipe and begins to smoke. Ten Bears watches him closely.

TEN BEARS
Dances With Wolves is quiet these days.

He does not reply. He smokes a little more and passes the pipe.

TEN BEARS
Is his heart bad?

Dances With Wolves glances at the men around the fire.

DANCES WITH WOLVES
Killing the soldiers at the river was a good thing.
It made me free, and my heart was big to see my
friends coming to help me. I did not mind killing
those men. I was glad to do it.

He searches for the right words.

DANCES WITH WOLVES
But the soldiers hate me now like they hate no
other. They think I am a traitor. They will hunt for
me. And when they find me, they will find you. I
think it would be wise to move the village.

There is a murmur around the fire. He has difficulty
going on.

DANCES WITH WOLVES
I must go . . . I must try and talk to those who
would listen.

Objections break out all around the fire. Wind In His Hair
jumps to his feet, and even Kicking Bird is protesting.

TEN BEARS
Quiet! You are hurting my ears. . . . Leave us alone.

When he and Dances With Wolves are alone, Ten Bears
speaks again.

TEN BEARS

You are the only white man I have ever known. I
have thought about you a lot. More than you know.

But I think you are wrong. The man the soldiers
are looking for no longer exists. Now there is only a
Sioux named Dances With Wolves.

Let's smoke awhile. . .

DUNBAR (INTERNAL)

*"With Ten Bears it was always more than awhile. There
was purpose in everything he did, and I knew he wanted me
to stay. But I was sure of myself. I would be an excuse, and
that was all the Army would need to find this place.*

*"I pushed him as far as I could to move the camp. But
in the end he only smiled and talked of simple pleasures.
He reminded me that at his age, a good fire is better
than anything."*

Dances With Wolves had guessed right. Already, a large column of
soldiers led by the same major who had imprisoned him was making
their way toward the snow-covered mountains. They were guided by
Pawnee scouts.

Dances With Wolves and Stands With A Fist made their final
preparations for departure. It was a painful time, not just for them
but for the entire village, and especially his closest friends.

Dances With Wolves finished the pipe he had been making as a
parting gift for Kicking Bird, and went in search of him. They met
outside on the path running through the village.

[Winter camp]
Gradually they realize that each has selected the same

parting gift. It's heartbreaking. Kicking Bird tries to cover with a casual question, but it's all fake.

> KICKING BIRD
> You've finished your pipe? How does it smoke?

> DANCES WITH WOLVES
> I've never smoked it.

He moves to make the exchange. Kicking Bird does the same. From one hand to the other. Men couldn't be closer.

> KICKING BIRD
> We have come far . . . you and me.

You were the first man I ever wanted to be like. I
will not forget you.

They were ready to leave, and none too soon. The Army's Pawnee
scouts had picked up the trail leading to the winter camp. The soldiers
quickened their pace and made ready for battle.

Just as they were finished packing their ponies, Smiles A Lot
approached tentatively, for once not smiling. He handed Dances With
Wolves a leather-wrapped bundle. Opening it in puzzlement, Dances
With Wolves found his water-stained journal, which the boy had spied
floating by and fished out of the river on the day of the rescue.

Dances With Wolves and Stands With A Fist mounted their ponies
and slowly rode through the village, leading their pack horse. The other
Sioux went through the motions of going about their work as usual,
but the silence in camp was profound.

[Canyon trail]
They have reached the head of the trail leading out of the
winter camp. Just as they begin to ascend, a voice, calling
from afar, brings them to a halt. The sound echoes through
the canyons, through the village.

WIND IN HIS HAIR
(calling) Dances With Wolves . . .

He and his pony are perched on a ledge high up near the
canyon rim. His pony is jacked up and, as always, Wind
In His Hair looks the perfect warrior. But now his face is
full of stress as he screams out the message he could not
deliver in person.

WIND IN HIS HAIR
I am Wind In His Hair . . .

Everyone in the camp has stopped to listen.

> WIND IN HIS HAIR
> Can you not see that I am your friend? . . .

Dances With Wolves looks ready to crack.

> WIND IN HIS HAIR
> Can you not see that you will always be my friend?

Dances With Wolves lets the unhappy echo of these words fade away before he starts his pony again.

It is dusk, and troops are moving quietly through the trees along the canyon trail, sabers drawn.

The rest of the troops have moved to the edge of the canyon rim. They too are quiet. Down below, the Pawnee scouts are milling about, looking for sign.

The soldiers from the canyon floor are silently arriving on the scene. The Pawnee look to the lead scout on the canyon rim. They have no answer, and the lead scout has none to give the general at his side. Ten Bears' village is gone.

A great, yellow full moon has just appeared above the opposite rim of the canyon. The yellow is brilliant, a great spotlight of golden color.

A wolf steps into the light on the opposite rim. He's walking in the backdrop of the moon. The wolf suddenly arches his back, sticks his muzzle in the air, and produces a spine-tingling howl. The sound bounces all over the canyon and into the star-filled winter sky.

Dances With Wolves and Stands With A Fist continue up the canyon trail as the camera slowly pulls back.

Production Notes

Behind-the-Scenes Interviews with the Filmmakers and the Cast

To stage the Tennessee battle scene, 250 Civil War reenactors were brought in—organized groups that regularly put on reenactments of Civil War engagements, complete with costumes and horses.

Jeffrey Beecroft, the production designer, remembers some of the challenges of shooting the Civil War scenes:

"These scenes were supposed to take place in the fall, but logistically we couldn't shoot in the fall. So what we did was literally to paint the season in, using about 10,000 gallons of paint. Painting the cornstalks yellow.

And since we were shooting in South Dakota, painting the foliage on trees to resemble an Eastern autumn. The grass, on the other hand, was too brown there; that had to be dyed green. It was one of the biggest visual challenges of the film.

"The scale of the landscape set the tone. We didn't build studio sets; we built everything on location. The interiors are matched to the exteriors; they're one and the same. Locations mean plenty of logistical problems—you have to bring everything with you on a show like this; South Dakota doesn't have any prop houses."

Kevin Costner speaks about his new role as a director:

"As a director, you have to remind somebody what it's like to breathe, what it's like to be out of air. You have to remind him that someone's being killed two feet away from him. You have to remind him that the horse he's trying to get on represents life and death. If that helps the actor, I'm really glad to do it.

". . . I like the word 'action.' It describes what you want. You know, film isn't about doing as little as possible, it's about doing as much as you can, and then seeing how it translates. So 'action' is a good word for me.

"Someone told me, 'Look, there's no doubt you're going to stay up all night thinking about where you're going to put the camera the first time, to look like you know what you're doing.' But it's not where you set the camera down the first time that's the challenge. It's where do you put it the second time? And every time after that. It's how to sustain the imagination."

Before the shooting begins, storyboards are used to map out a director's vision of where the camera will be placed for major action sequences in a film.

To give Dances With Wolves *as much authenticity as possible, its creative designers during pre-production traveled throughout the West and Southwest gathering historical information. They also combed libraries, archives, and museums for rare pictures and objects.*

Production designer Jeff Beecroft:

"Kevin wanted to offer a reality that hasn't been seen on the screen before. He wanted to convey a West that was wild and untamed and larger than life, as seen through the eyes of Dunbar, who comes from the East.

"In working together, we broke the script down into a series of emotional moments—moments that made his character see things differently. We did that with one phrase or one feeling in each scene. For example, with Fort Sedgewick he wanted a sense of claustrophobia, because it's in the middle of nowhere, totally isolated. So we made this little island in the middle of nowhere, a sod house with ceilings six feet high so he had to stoop to enter."

"The painting on the horses was taken from old pictographs on tipi liners—those were a great source of designs—and each symbol is significant. Kicking Bird, the medicine man—his horse has a key symbol and a hailstorm. People in mourning have a hand wiped across the side. It all means something . . . and the Pawnee symbols are different from the Sioux."

The same painted symbols were often used to decorate both horse and rider. Some of them were:

War party leader

Enemy killed in hand combat

Owner fought from behind breastworks

Hail

Coup marks

Horse raids

Mourning marks

Medicine symbol

America's Fascinating Indian Heritage

The world's largest privately owned buffalo herd, some 3,500 strong, was in some way the "star" of Dances With Wolves. *Rancher Roy Houck's 32 years of experience with the animals proved invaluable in planning the film's awesome hunting sequences. Trucks and helicopters were brought in to herd and pace thousands of buffalo for the tricky procedure.*

Producer Jim Wilson says:

"Talk about logistics . . . Kevin from the get-go wanted it as big as it could possibly be, so we started with 3,000 buffalo—never before have that many been used in a given scene. The shooting took eight days, and we had a helicopter, ten pickups, twenty-four Indians riding bareback, and an additional twenty wranglers working with us."

Carefully monitored to avoid any misuse or harm, several trained animals were brought in to handle some of the more unusual special effects. Domesticated buffalo such as Cody and Mammoth (owned by rock singer Neil Young) were lent to the production for a scene during which the buffalo are supposedly struck by arrows, fall from a full run, and are trampled by other buffalo. In this case, the huge Mammoth was safely rigged with a strap to look as if arrows went through him. Articulated buffalo—essentially lookalikes built from wire and fur coverings—were used to portray the fallen animals.

Kevin Costner:

"The buffalo won a lot of respect—they're faster than horses, they run longer than horses, and they never backed down. They really fed our film, and in some way held it up spiritually.

"The very first day the buffalo ran, there were three thousand of them coming at us, and nobody was sure what was going to happen. The Native American riders were wild and they were great rodeo riders, but no one had ridden among the buffalo for more than a hundred years. So no one knew what to expect, really, and suddenly here they came over the hill, and people's stomachs were in their throats. . . .

"All of a sudden one buffalo started to bolt in the wrong direction, and that's when I knew these guys [the riders] were committed. Because they were afraid, but they threw their horses in front of those buffalo and tried to salvage that run. You saw their courage grow every day, and the whole thing got to an almost spiritual level.

"I think the realism has a lot to do with it. People watching the movie won't notice this unless they look hard, but all these guys are bareback, they're riding with traditional hackamores, and they were flying—really flying. They did it for themselves and they did it for something long ago that will never come again. They turned the clock around."

Producer Jim Wilson:

"Kevin and I are both perfectionists and hate nothing more than to see a fake on screen. He likes to do his own stunts as much as possible. And we shot in such a fine-grained film that anytime I put up my stunt man, as close a double as he is, I always knew it wasn't Kevin, and it bothered both of us. But it was certainly a fear of mine during the shooting, especially with him directing as well as starring. While everyone else was replaceable, the fact was that if Kevin went down, we'd all go down.

"All the riding in the buffalo sequence is Kevin himself. He was out there for eight days, riding bareback for a good half of the picture, shooting his gun without the reins. . . .

"So one day he did get knocked off his horse—the horse stumbled when another rider veered into him at full speed. I was up in the helicopter. The radio's crackling in my headphones, and I hear 'Action!' and then I hear 'He's down, he's down!' That was a bad moment."

Kevin Costner:

"But the great thing about that moment was that my stunt coordinator, Norman Howell, immediately bolted out and just said, 'How are you?' I said, 'I'm fine—give me your horse.' And he looked at me and just made the decision to do it, no more questions. Right in the middle of that chaos he calmly rebridled the horse in a split second so I could get back into the hunt."

The language spoken by the Sioux people in the film is Lakota, one of several Sioux dialects. This native language was nearly lost in the government's attempt to assimilate the tribes. Few people speak it today, but community colleges on the reservations have recently begun teaching it to younger people again.

The producers were fortunate in having the assistance of Doris Leader Charge, an instructor of Lakota language and culture at Sinte Gleska College on the Rosebud Reservation. Doris translated the screenplay dialogue and served as a coach and technical advisor during the shooting, conducting a three-week "crash *course" for the principal actors. Kevin Costner and Mary McDonnell needed tutoring, of course, but so did most of the Indian actors, who—with the exception of Floyd Westerman (Ten Bears)—belonged to tribes other than the Sioux.*

Doris also appears in Dances With Wolves, *playing the role of Pretty Shield, the wife of chief Ten Bears.*

"Lakota is a very difficult language with so many strange sounds," explains Leader Charge. "We had to first translate the script the way we would speak it, then go back and simplify the dialogue, using fewer and easier words with similar meanings.

"The first contact I had with the movie was a call from Jim Wilson, asking if we could translate the script and could he send a copy out— did Federal Express come to the reservation? When we translated, we also recorded each actor's part on tape, so they could practice it on their own.

"The young boys who play Smiles A Lot, Otter, and Worm are also Sioux—Ehasa, that's Smiles A Lot, is from my reservation—but they were never taught their language. It was forbidden by the Bureau of Indian Affairs for many generations, until

the Freedom of Religion Act was passed in the 1970s. They figured if they outlawed our language and ceremonies, we'd become assimilated—but it never really happened.

"My Grandma was around at the time of the Wounded Knee massacre, and she taught me the traditional ways, though we had to sneak around to do it. We used to walk five miles, way down a canyon where a medicine man lived, to pray. She told me not to ever give that up because if we ever lost our language and our culture, we would lose everything.

"We don't call ourselves Sioux— that name was given to us by other tribes. It's actually a longer word with 'Sioux' at the end, and it means Poison Otter, because anyone who got in our way might be in trouble. We were a warring tribe and believed in fighting for what was ours. I guess you might say we're still trying to do that with the Black Hills. Anyway, that's where the name Sioux came from; we call ourselves Lakotas. 'Lakota' means 'allies,' in the sense of family.

"I was scared about doing this movie at the beginning, but it's been a good experience. It portrays us as we really are. They've gotten it right this time."

Mary McDonnell, who plays the pivotal role of Stands With A Fist, is best known on the New York stage.

Kevin Costner talks about why she was cast in the part:
"We saw a lot of actresses, and there were several strong candidates among better-known film actresses, but Mary brought so much to the role that we wanted. For one thing, I felt that having a face people had seen over and over would take something away from the magic of this story.

"But the key word in characterizing Stands With A Fist was 'woman,' not girl. I wanted someone with lines on her face, and that's not an easy thing to explain to a studio.

"She became a leader on the set, too. She was a powerful presence; everyone recognized in her a person who has invested her life in acting. A lot of the other actors fell into step with that."

Mary McDonnell comments:
"It was sad to realize that I'd heard less of a Native American language than of almost any language on the planet. The sounds were so unfamiliar to me and put together in unfamiliar ways, so it was frightening at the beginning. But we had a great teacher in Doris: she was very clear about how to go about it. And I suppose as an actress I'm used to picking up languages and sounds."

Tantoo Cardinal portrays Kicking Bird's wife, Black Shawl. Raised in northern Canada, she is a métis, or mixed blood—part Cree and part Chippewa.

"My great-grandfather was a member of Big Bear's tribe, one of the last in northern Canada to sign treaties.

"Our way of understanding life, our concept of the earth as a living being, was alien to the people who came here. They knew so much, they didn't have anything to learn from us. And that gave them permission to see us as ignorant.

"People came to North America for religious freedom, and where did the land come from to live on? From people who are persecuted. Our children were taken away and put in boarding schools so they wouldn't grow up to be Indian. Our language was outlawed; we were not allowed to pray in the Indian way, or wear Indian clothing, or live in the Indian way. That was a conscious thing: we have to make these people into white people.

"Maybe in their own way they were saying, our way of life is good and you should have that. But it was not love that did those things. When your spiritual freedom is taken away, that's the water of your soul."

Graham Greene, who plays the medicine man Kicking Bird, is a full-blooded Oneida, one of the Iroquois tribes, born on the Six Nations Reserve in Ontario, Canada. He is a seasoned professional with many film and television credits, and is also active in the Toronto theatre.

Kevin Costner says:
"Graham was a real score, a talented actor who was able to bring a lot of himself to the role. He doesn't come off right away as a strong Indian 'type,' so at first I saw just the professional actor rather than some sculpted guy that maybe I was looking for. But his low-key style fit the character."

Screenwriter Michael Blake adds:
"Graham is a good example of how this movie was cast—the Indians are human beings first, not just types. You see it in his first appearance at the fort, when he just walks around calmly and thoughtfully checking things out. He doesn't creep around like an aborigine, but like he's taking a stroll in the park. That's Graham: very poised. Then he speaks in Lakota to Dunbar's horse, and suddenly he's in another dimension.

That made him an Indian—but he'd already established his personality first."

Graham Greene:
"I was brought up without much sense of my Indian heritage, and now I'm slowly learning what my people were and the traditions behind them. My tribe was one of the Six Nations of the Iroquois Confederacy, which had a very sophisticated structure and political system. Ben Franklin, bless his little soul and his kite, used the Confederacy as a model for the U.S. Constitution.

"There was a real Kicking Bird, a Kiowa chief, that Michael based his character on. He did believe that the country was going to be overrun with white people, and believed that he should create a liaison with the whites so they could live together— but his people didn't like that, and the story goes that he was eventually killed because of it."

"The medicine man was a spiritual force and also an herbalist—sort of a combination GP and psychiatrist. Sometimes those two functions were handled by different people. He would care for his people in many ways—their mental welfare, their future, interpreting signs about what might happen to them, guiding them in consultation with the other elders.

"I've talked to some medicine men, and most of them are well into their seventies. Yet the first thing they say to you when you want to know something is, 'I'm just a child myself, I'm still a baby.' "

The Kiowa chief Kicking Bird, left, was the model for Graham Greene's character.

Elsa Zamparelli, costume designer:

"All the Indian actors are wearing their own eagle feathers, for a very good reason. We're not allowed to use them, because eagles are endangered. But it's legal for the Indians to have them, and in a lot of cases they've been passed down from older family members."

"Kevin's supposed to become very slowly more Indian, and as he does so, he sheds more of his white man clothing. But he wanted to maintain the idea of combining both aspects of his character, so he said, I always want to wear my military pants and boots."

The venerable chief Ten Bears is played by Native American actor, activist, and folk singer Floyd Red Crow Westerman. Born on a Dakota Sioux reservation in South Dakota, Westerman has made many film and TV appearances, and recorded two folk albums. He tours widely as a singer in support of human rights for indigenous peoples, including a recent worldwide tour with Sting and the Amazon chief Raoni, for the Rain Forest Foundation Project. As a leader in the North American Indian movement, he is actively involved in working for the recognition of treaty, land, and religious rights.

"A lot of my memories from when I was a little boy center around the tribal celebrations, the powwows. I'd spend all my energy running around with the other kids where everyone was dancing, and then go to sleep in the tent to the sound of the drum beating all night long. Anytime you woke up in the night, you would hear the drum and go back to sleep. So that's still a beautiful sound for me, and it's always a good feeling to go back to those celebrations.

"Around the 1960s and '70s, a lot of interest came back in holding the ceremonies and rediscovering the traditions. Simple things like the burning of sage in the household every day. . . . Later in life you begin to find reasons why such things have always been and always should be.

"Near the end of the film we smoke the pipe—that's one of the greatest ceremonies. When we share the pipe, the smoke carries our thoughts to the Great Spirit as it goes up. And the pipe bowl is the center of the people. So it's very important when this is shared—it means the person you are sharing it with is someone you have confidence in, someone you accept and adopt into your family, and take into your life.

"Before the time of the Christian, most of our culture was living by the rivers and moving out into the prairies to hunt, then back into the winter camps at the river bottoms. That lifestyle is very old. People have been traced back on this continent fifty thousand winters.

"The last massacre was only a hundred winters ago. I was born forty-six winters ago. So in terms of time that is very short. Think about fifty thousand winters . . . then you have a deeper understanding of what kind of culture it took to survive. I think this is an important film to show the world the reality of how it was then."

Rodney Grant is an Omaha, raised on the Omaha Tribal Reservation in Nebraska. He has played roles in several Native American-themed movies.

"A warrior like Wind In His Hair is the spirit and backbone of the community. He wins respect by displaying courage, by defending his people, by showing good moral character.

"My tribe, the Omaha, were not a warring tribe. Our reservation is on the Missouri River, where we've been for a long time. People coming up and down the river would stop and visit the Omaha because they were known to be a generous people.

"I was one of those who chose to surrender their heritage when I was young—I thought, what do we need that for? We're a new generation; we need to learn the white man's ways to survive. But to survive you need both worlds. You need an identity, your inner self who you actually are. And I guess if you say you're Indian, then you've got to know what 'Indian' is.

"The world Dunbar comes from is very different from the Indian world. In his soldier world, respect is measured by the rank you achieve. In our world a warrior doesn't have stripes, he doesn't have a title—his name and his abilities are his stripes. The things he's accomplished in life make the man, not what he wears on his sleeve.

"What Dances With Wolves learns from Wind In His Hair is what it's like to have people depend on you. To have the spirit, the drive, to take a group of people and move them forward into their life."

Producer Jim Wilson:

"One of the things we heard from a lot of people was 'Don't use wolves.' They're one of the most difficult animals to work with, and ours ran true to form—but I really didn't think we could get away with not using them.

"We looked at a lot of film of half-breeds, malamutes, huskies. And though they may look like a wolf, they don't *walk* like a wolf. Wolves have a very distinctive way of walking on those long, thin legs, and the wolf lope is unmistakable.

"There's just something about it when they look at you and the camera catches them just right—a glint in the eye—a true wildness that was worth all the frustration. To name the picture *Dances With Wolves* and not use real wolves I think would have been a travesty."

"An Indian . . . might be named for an animal, for a physical phenomenon such as thunder that occurred on the day of birth, or even for a brave deed that had once been performed by the giver of the name. A woman generally kept the name she was given at birth, but a man often replaced his original name with a new one that celebrated a personal act of valor, recalled an encounter with an unusual animal, or perhaps was inspired by a dream."

The Indians

For Further Reading

Compiled and Annotated by Michael Blake

Black Elk, *Black Elk Speaks: Being the Life Story of a Holy Man of the Oglala Sioux*. Edited by John G. Neihardt. Lincoln: University of Nebraska Press, 1932, 1979.

One of a handful of sacred books written in this century.

Brown, Dee. *Bury My Heart at Wounded Knee: An Indian History of the American West*. New York: Henry Holt & Company, 1971.

The first book to get at the truth of what really happened. A milestone.

Connell, Evan S. *Son of the Morning Star: Custer and the Little Bighorn*. Berkeley, CA: North Point Press, 1984.

A seminal book about Custer and the Little Bighorn, exquisitely written.

Cremony, John C. *Life Among the Apaches*. Lincoln: University of Nebraska Press, 1983.

A first-person account, full of color and pathos.

Eastlake, William. *Go In Beauty*. Albuquerque: University of New Mexico Press, 1980.

An epic story by a Nobel-caliber writer.

Erdoes, Richard, and Ortiz, Alfonso, eds. *American Indian Myths and Legends*. New York: Pantheon Books, 1984.

A bountiful collection of Native American folktales gathered from all over the continent, with superb commentaries.

Hoig, Stan. *The Battle of the Washita: The Sheridan-Custer Indian Campaign of 1867-69*. Lincoln: University of Nebraska Press, 1976.

A great scholar's version of controversial events.

Irving, Washington. *A Tour of the Prairies* (1835). Reprint. New York: Pantheon Books, 1967.

The creator of Rip Van Winkle and Ichabod Crane gives us a personalized look at the frontier in the 1830s.

Mails, Thomas E. *The Mystic Warriors of the Plains*. New York: Doubleday, 1972.

The work of a lifetime in one volume. Reverent and incredibly informative.

Marriot, Alice. *Kiowa Years*. New York: Macmillan, 1967.

The last days of the free Kiowas, told with care and clarity and deep respect.

Nye, Wilbur Sturtevant. *Plains Indian Raiders*. Norman: University of Oklahoma Press, 1968.

An excellent book with spectacular photographs by William Soule.

Sandoz, Mari. *Crazy Horse—The Strange Man of the Oglalas*. Lincoln: University of Nebraska Press, 1968.

He might have been the greatest American ever. A beautiful and moving book.

_____. *These Were the Sioux*. Lincoln: University of Nebraska Press, 1961.

A small treasure containing volumes of insight.

Spotts, David L. *Campaigning with Custer 1868-1869*. Lincoln: University of Nebraska Press, 1988.

Spotts was there and tells his story in the form of a fresh, unpretentious diary.

Waters, Frank. *The Man Who Killed the Deer*. New York: Washington Square Press, 1980.

A true classic of fiction that leaps the boundaries of genre.

"Dances With Wolves" Official Cast and Credits Roll

CAST

Lieutenant Dunbar	KEVIN COSTNER
Stands with a Fist	MARY McDONNELL
Kicking Bird	GRAHAM GREENE
Wind In His Hair	RODNEY A. GRANT
Ten Bears	FLOYD RED CROW WESTERMAN
Black Shawl	TANTOO CARDINAL
Timmons	ROBERT PASTORELLI
Lieutenant Elgin	CHARLES ROCKET
Major Fambrough	MAURY CHAYKIN
Stone Calf	JIMMY HERMAN
Smiles A Lot	NATHAN LEE CHASING HIS HORSE
Otter	MICHAEL SPEARS
Worm	JASON R. LONE HILL
Spivey	TONY PIERCE
Pretty Shield	DORIS LEADER CHARGE
Sergeant Pepper	TOM EVERETT
Sergeant Bauer	LARRY JOSHUA
Edwards	KIRK BALTZ
Major	WAYNE GRACE
General Tide	DONALD HOTTON
Christine	ANNIE COSTNER
Willie	CONOR DUFFY
Christine's Mother	ELISA DANIEL
Big Warrior	PERCY WHITE PLUME
Escort Warrior	JOHN TAIL
Sioux #1/Warrior #1	STEVE REEVIS
Sioux #2/Warrior #2	SHELDON WOLFCHILD
Toughest Pawnee	WES STUDI
Pawnee #1	BUFFALO CHILD
Pawnee #2	CLAYTON BIG EAGLE
Pawnee #3	RICHARD LEADER CHARGE
Sioux Warriors	REDWING TED NEZ
	MARVIN HOLY
Sioux Courier	RAYMOND NEWHOLY
Kicking Bird's Son	DAVID J. FULLER
Kicking Bird's Eldest Son	RYAN WHITE BULL
Kicking Bird's Daughter	OTAKUYE CONROY
Village Mother	MARETTA BIG CROW
Guard	STEVE CHAMBERS
General's Aide	WILLIAM H. BURTON
Confederate Cavalryman	BILL W. CURRY
Confederate Soldiers	NICK THOMPSON
	CARTER HANNER
Wagon Driver	KENT HAYS
Union Soldier	ROBERT GOLDMAN
Tucker	FRANK P. COSTANZA
Ray	JAMES A. MITCHELL
Ambush Wagon Driver	R.L. CURTIN
Cisco	JUSTIN
Two Socks	TEDDY & BUCK

CREDITS

Directed By	KEVIN COSTNER
Produced By	JIM WILSON and KEVIN COSTNER
Executive Producer	JAKE EBERTS
Screenplay By	MICHAEL BLAKE
	Based On His Novel
Edited By	NEIL TRAVIS, A.C.E.
Director of Photography	DEAN SEMLER, A.C.S.
Production Designer	JEFFREY BEECROFT
Costume Designer	ELSA ZAMPARELLI
Music Composed and Conducted by	JOHN BARRY
Casting by	ELISABETH LEUSTIG, C.S.A.
Associate Producer	BONNIE ARNOLD
Unit Prodn Manager/Line Producer	DEREK KAVANAGH
First Assistant Director	DOUGLAS C. METZGER
Second Assistant Director	STEPHEN P. DUNN
Assistants to Kevin Costner	ALLISON CONANT
	GREGORY AVELLONE
Second 2nd Assistant Director	LINDA J. BRACHMAN
DGA Trainee	DAVID A. FUDGE
Staff Assistants	DAVID SILVA SEAN KAVANAGH
Art Director	WM LADD SKINNER
Set Decorator	LISA DEAN
Set Dressers	DAYNA LEE
	PAUL AURTHER HARTMAN
On Set Dressers	DWAIN F. WILSON
	STEVEN K. BARNETT
Leadman	PATRICK T. CASSIDY
Editors	WILLIAM HOY
	STEPHEN POTTER CHIP MASAMITSU
Assistant Editor	ROBERT C. LUSTED
Apprentice Editor	ERIC O. SCHUSTERMAN
Script Supervisor	JAN EVANS
Still Photographer	BEN GLASS
Camera Operator	JAMES MURO
First Assistant Cameramen	LEE BLASINGAME
	MARK DAVISON
Second Assistant Cameraman	DUDLEY J. VOLL
Loader	LEIGH FEITELBERG
Shotmaker Operator	CHRIS SUMMERELL
Steadicam Cinematographer	JAMES MURO
Video Playback Operator	BLAIR FORWARD
Production Sound Mixers	RUSSELL WILLIAMS, C.A.S.
	MARY JO DEVENNEY
Boom Operator	ALBERTO AQUINO
Cableman	LEE LOESCH
Swing Gang Foreman	JEFF HARTMANN
Swing Gang	JAMES A. BRADLEY
	DARRYL HAYES JAY B. CURRY
Production Coordinator	DORIS HARTLEY

Production Secretary ....STACEY HARTLEY
Assistant Production Coordinator ....LYNNE FERRY
Set Costumer ....BARBARA GORDON
Costume Construction ....CATHY SMITH
Costume Supervisor ....BIRGITTA BJERKE
Assistant Costume Supervisor ....JULIA GOMBERT
Costume Assistant ....RON BEEBE
Chief Makeup ....FRANK CARRISOSA
Key Makeup ....DAVID ATHERTON
1st Assistant Makeup ....PATRICIA CARRISOSA
Assistant Makeup ....TAMMY ASHMORE
TEA JAY GLASS KARIN HAYES TERRI GOETT
Chief Hairstylist ....ELLE ELLIOTT
Key Hairstylist ....TAMARA GUTHRIE
Hairstylist ....JOANI YARBROUGH
Assistant Hairstylists ....HEATHER MATISOFF
DEBORAH MILLS-GUSMANO BETH MILLER
LINDA BOWMAN LINDA PETERSON
2nd Unit Directed by ....JOHN HUNECK
& PHILIP C. PFEIFFER
Additional Camera Operators ....S. PHILLIP SPARKS
Assistant Cameramen ....FRED I. McLANE
HENRY TIRL JOSEPH SANCHEZ
JIMMY JENSEN
2nd Unit Script Supervisor ....ANGELA ROBINSON
Location Manager ....TIM WILSON
Assistant Location Managers ....H. JANE NAUMAN
CHRIS A. HIPPLE
Greens Supervisor ....STEPHANIE WALDRON
Greens Laborers ....CHARLES FOGG
PAUL CLARK
Standby Greens ....BRAD BOOTH
Property Master ....SCOTT A. STEPHENS
Assistant Property Master ....JOHN CAMERON
Second Assistant Propmasters ....IVICA BILICH
CHARLES BLUDSWORTH
Props Assistant ...........................J.R. KUSSMAN
Illustrators ....STEVE BURG
LEONARD MORGANTI
Model Maker ....ANDREW PRECHT
Wagon Master ....CINDY COSTNER
Wagon Supplier.........................LAVON SHEARER
Stunt Coordinator ....NORMAN L. HOWELL
Stand-Ins ....MARK THOMASON
DON ROBINSON BRENDA J. CARROLL
Head Wrangler/Trainer ....RUSTY HENDRICKSON
Wranglers ....RICK WYANT
SCOTTY AUGARE DUTCH LUNAK
R.L. CURTIN BOB FRICKSON
INGRID "TILLY" SEMLER ROY VAVRA
Small Animal Wranglers ....S. FOX SLOAN
DAN WESSON
Wolf Trainers ....PAUL "SLED" REYNOLDS
GAYLE PHELPS
Additional Wolf Trainers ...."LIVING LEGENDS"
FRED & ALUNE DUBRAY
Bison Consultants ....ROY HOUCK
DUANE LAMMERS

Casting Assistant...............................SUSAN BROWN
Extras Casting ....RENE HAYNES
Extras Casting Assistants.....DARLENE "KA MOOK" NICHOLS
CATHERINE "KITTY" DUFFY
Historic Re-enactment Coordinator...........ANDY CANNON
Sound Design ....ROBERT FITZGERALD
Sound Editing .........................SOUNDBUSTERS
Supervising Sound Editors.........................HARI RYATT
ROBERT FITZGERALD
Sound Editors ....BRUCE STUBBLEFIELD
LINDA MOSS ALBERT GASSER
JEFF ROSEN HOWARD GINDOFF ED FASSL
Supervising ADR Editor ....BARBARA BARNABY
ADR Editor ....CHRIS JARGO
Assistant ADR Editor ....GINA SPIRO
Group ADR Cordinator .... BURTON SHARP
ADR Mixer ....DOC KANE
Foley Artists ....DAN O'CONNELL
ALICIA STEVENSON
Foley Mixer ....TIM HOGGAT
Foley Editors .... JOHN DUVALL
JOEL BERKOVITZ
Assistant Sound Editors ....JUSTINE TURNER
RUBEN DOMINGO
Music Supervisor ....JOHN COINMAN
Music Editor ....CLIF KOHLWECK
Re-Recording by...........INTERNATIONAL RECORDING
CORPORATION
Supervising Re-Recording Mixer............. JEFFREY PERKINS
Re-Recording Mixer ....BILL BENTON
GREG WATKINS ANDY NAPELL
Recordist ....LARRY HOKI
Music Scoring Mixer........................SHAWN MURPHY
Scoring Recordist.........................SUSAN MCLEAN
Orchestrator ....GREIG MCRICHIE
Additional Music "Fire Dance" ....PETER BUFFETT
Traditional Music by ....PORCUPINE SINGERS
Chief Special Effects...........................ROBBIE KNOTT
1st Assistant Special Effects.................... JOHN K. STIRBER
Special Effects Assistants....................JOSEPH E. KNOTT
MICHAEL BOLAN
Mechanical Animal Effects
Created by ....KNB EFFECTS GROUP
Buffalo Effects Supervisors ....ROBERT KURTZMAN
GREG NICOTERO HOWARD BERGER
SHANNON SHEA
Construction Coordinator ....BEN ZELLER
Construction Foremen ....JIM HILL
AL EYLAR
Shop Foreman ....BOB STURTEVANT
Crew Boss ....CARL ZELLER
Foremen-Fort Hayes ....DAVE BEST
THOMAS MICHAEL RYAN
Local Foremen ....MONTE CURRY
BILL DEYONGE
Mill Man ....DAVE RODEN
Labor Foreman ....DAWNA GRAVATT

Carpenters ....PATRICK MOLLMAN
REED A. FINCH KERRY J. FROSH
Standby Carpenters ....MARVIN HOLY
ROBERT DES JARLAIS
Gaffer ....VICTOR PEREZ
Best Boy Electric ....MARC WOSTAK
Electricians ....MICHAEL BLUNDELL
RAYMOND GONZALES
Key Grip ....WILLIAM "BEAR" PAUL
Best Boy Grip ....KIM HEATH
Dolly Grip ....JOHN MURPHY
Grips ....WILLIAM EDWARD PAUL
MIKE DUNSON DOUG COWDEN
BRYON BOWER TONY DEVITO LYLE EHLERS
Head Scenic Painter ....WARD WELTON
Lead Painter ....RON ASHMORE
Scenic Painters ....RICHARD PUGA
JIM STEERE
Standby Scenic Painter ....PATRICK S. THOMS
Transportation Coordinator ....DAVID SIEGEL
Transportation Captain ....JONATHAN ROSENFELD
Transportation Co-Captain ....WAYNE JONES
Unit Publicist ....PETER W. HAAS
International Publicist ....TRISTAN WHALLEY
Production Accountant ....JOHN T. HAUN
Assistant Accountants ....THOMAS A. DAVILA
DAWN RENAE SCHMITZ
Post Production Accounting ....PREP SHOOT POST
Post Production Accountant ....CHRIS ROMBERG
Production Assistants ....EDWARD GORSUCH
FRAN L. WELLS MARK EILERS
DONNA BOND SANDERS RHONDA S. RICHARDS
TOM BYRNES JACQUELINE C. JOHNSON
BETH ANN IRION LYNDA DONAHUE
KYMBERLY JENKINS MOIRA MCLAUGHLIN
TERRY ALBRIGHT
Craft Service ....TUTT A. ESQUERRE
TIM HILL STEVEN ZUKOWSKI
First Aid ....JAY IVERS
DR. RICHARD WAGNER
Caterer ....FOR STARS CATERING
Lakota Translator/
Dialogue Coach ....DORIS LEADER CHARGE
ALBERT WHITE HAT
Video Documentarian ....TIM MERRILL
Technical Advisors ....CATHY SMITH
LARRY BELITZ
Matte Painting Crew ....MATTHEW YURICICH
ROCCO GIOFFRE
Matte Camera Crew ....ROBERT BAILEY
PAUL CURLEY
Helicopter Pilot ....GARY E. PFAFF
Completion Guarantee Provided by .....THE COMPLETION
BOND COMPANY, INC.
Negative Cutter ....GARY BURRITT
Main Title Artwork by ....MATSUNO DESIGN GROUP
Titles and Optical Effects by ....CINEMA RESEARCH
CORPORATION

Title Design ....DAVID L. AARON
JAY JOHNSON
Color by De Luxe®
Color Timer.................................MIKE STANWICK

Special Thanks To
The Spirited People of South Dakota
who helped make this film possible
Roy Houck and Kay Ingles - Triple U Standing Butte Ranch
777 Bison Ranch Sioux Indian Nation
The Honorable Governor and Mrs. George S. Mickelson
Gary Keller and the South Dakota Film Commission
Black Hills National Forest Homestake Mining Company
South Dakota Law Enforcement
South Dakota Department of Game, Fish & Parks
Badlands National Park Indian Learning Center
Storm Mountain Center South Dakota Job Services
Pierre and Rapid City Chambers of Commerce
Verendrye Museum
Institute of Range and the American Mustang
Mule Utility Vehicles by Kawasaki U.S.A.
West River Video Productions
and Kevin Reynolds
Every effort was made to ensure the safety of all the animals
depicted in the film. All the featured animals were trained
and handled by professional animal specialists.

TIG Productions Inc. is the author of this motion picture
for purposes of Article 15 (2) of the Berne convention and
all national laws giving effect thereto.
The story, all names, characters and incidents portrayed in this
production are fictitious. No identification with or similarity to
actual persons, living or dead, or to actual events is intended or
should be inferred.

An Orion Pictures Release, U.S. and Canada
Majestic Films International, All Other Countries

About the Authors

MICHAEL BLAKE, who adapted the screenplay for "Dances With Wolves" from his novel of the same name, based his book on ten years of reading about and researching frontier history. Born in Fayetteville, North Carolina, Blake is a fourth-generation writer, whose great-grandfather fought in the Apache wars. His first produced screenplay was "Stacy's Knights," which introduced him to future collaborators Kevin Costner and Jim Wilson. *Dances With Wolves* was originally issued in paperback by Ballantine Books in 1988, and the hardcover edition was published in 1991 by Newmarket Press. The novel has now been translated into seventeen languages. Blake's second novel, *Airman Mortensen*, is published by Seven Wolves.

BEN GLASS is an actor turned photographer with an extensive background in theater arts, having earned a B.A. in theater at the University of Houston and directed several plays there and elsewhere. He turned to photography while studying acting at Trinity Square Rep in Rhode Island, shooting publicity portraits, and continued to pursue commercial photography along with acting in Los Angeles. He co-produced a feature film called "Hollywood Dreaming" with Jim Wilson, who later hired him to photograph "Dances With Wolves," his first major location assignment. Since then he has shot still photographs on location for "Young Guns II" and other major feature films.

JIM WILSON, producer with Kevin Costner, graduated from Antioch College and the Berkeley Film Institute (where he met writer Michael Blake). He founded American Twist Productions, where he produced and directed numerous short films for such clients as the U.S. Tennis Association, Volvo, and Kodak. His first feature film was directing "Stacy's Knights," in which he worked with Blake and Kevin Costner for the first time, and he later produced the video feature "Laughing Horse" (1984) and directed "The Movie Maker" (1986). He recently served as associate producer on "Revenge," starring Kevin Costner, with whom he is partnered in their Tig Productions. Wilson is also a founder of the Los Angeles Directors Workshop.

DANCES WITH WOLVES BOOKS FROM NEWMARKET PRESS

Newmarket Press is the official movie tie-in publisher for *Dances With Wolves*. Ask for these books at your local bookstore or order from Newmarket Press, 18 East 48th Street, New York, NY 10017 (212) 832-3575.

Dances With Wolves: The Illustrated Story of the Epic Film
Kevin Costner, Michael Blake, & Jim Wilson. Photos by Ben Glass.
The topselling illustrated moviebook of all time includes screenplay, production notes, the complete credit roll, editorial and art features on Native Americans, the frontier, the Civil War, and exclusive introductions by the authors.
(160 pp; 8 3/8" x 10 7/8"; 170 photos and drawings, 80 in color)
_____ hardcover, $29.95
_____ large format paperback, $16.95

Dances With Wolves: The Illustrated Screenplay and Story Behind the Film
(digest version)
An abridged edition of the bestselling moviebook, this low-priced reprint includes the complete screenplay, 16 pages of production notes, the credits, over 40 b&w photos and drawings. (144 pp.; 5 3/16" x 8")
_____ digest paperback, $4.95

Dances With Wolves: A Story for Children
Adapted by James Howe, based on the Michael Blake screenplay.
For all ages--a children's version of the now classic story of John Dunbar's life on the frontier among the Indians, illustrated with 68 color photos from the movie. (64 pp.; 8 3/8" x 10 7/8")
_____ hardcover (jacketed), $14.95

Dances With Wolves--The Novel
Michael Blake
The original novel that was the inspiration and basis for the award-winning movie, with a new afterword by the author. (336 pp; 5 1/2" x 8 1/4")
_____ hardcover (jacketed), $18.95

For postage and handling add $2.00 for the first book, plus $1.00 for each additional book thereafter. Please allow 4 to 6 weeks for delivery. Prices and availability are subject to change.

I am enclosing a check or money order payable to NEWMARKET PRESS, in the amount of $_____.

Name_____

Address_____

City/State_____

For quotes on special quantity purchase discounts, or for a copy of our catalog, please write or call the Newmarket Press Special Sales Department.